The Anglo Concertina Music of
Alan Day

Gary Coover

ROLLSTON PRESS

The Anglo Concertina Music of Alan Day
by Gary Coover

All rights reserved. No part of this book may be reproduced, scanned, transmitted, or distributed in any printed or electronic form without the prior permission of the author except in the case of brief quotations embodied in articles or reviews.

Copyright © 2024 Gary Coover

ISBN-13: 978-1-953208-18-7

All titles are in the public domain unless otherwise noted.

Interior photos provided by Alan Day

Also from Rollston Press: The Anglo Concertina Music of John Watcham (2020)
    The Anglo Concertina Music of John Kirkpatrick (2021)
    The Anglo Concertina Music of Phil Ham (2022)

ROLLSTON PRESS
1717 Ala Wai Blvd #1703
Honolulu, HI 96815
USA
info@rollstonpress.com

Preface

I first learned of Alan through his posts on concertina.net and videos on YouTube, as well as through his work in producing the landmark 3-CD sets of *Anglo International!* and *English International!*.

Although we had corresponded off and on for several years, I finally managed to meet up with Al in person at the historic Sutton Hoo site in Suffolk in late 2023. We quickly struck up a friendship over lunch and even ended up playing tunes in the National Trust parking lot!

And then it suddenly occurred to me – the world needed a book of Alan's tunes.

Transcribing his tunes has been a pleasure, and it has led me to believe that he is one of the most underrated concertina players playing today in the harmonic style. Alan's melodies and harmonies are absolutely lovely and are a joy to play, and he often varies the melodies and accompaniments each time he plays through the tunes. Many are very French sounding, undoubtedly from Alan's years of playing French music in the acclaimed band Rosbif. Of the 65 tunes in this book, 46 were composed by Alan.

In 2007, Peter Trimming recorded 7 videos of Alan's solo playing along with 6 videos of music sessions at the George Inn, Southwark, London. Alan began posting videos of his own playing on YouTube in 2011 at the age of 71. All of Alan's recordings are a one off take, and there is no double or multi tracking on the recordings. Many of the tunes in this book have been transcribed from those videos, and they can be accessed via scannable QR code links next to each tune.

Alan has done so much over the years to promote and encourage players of the concertina, it is indeed an honor and a privilege to be able to showcase his music.

If you enjoy playing the Anglo concertina in the harmonic style, then you are in for a treat. These are now some of my favorite tunes to play!

Gary Coover

Editor/Publisher
Rollston Press

Table of Contents

Introduction	9
The Anglo and Alan	10
Keyboard & Tablature	14
The Old Concertina	15
The Abigail Waltz	16
Adieu Sweet Lovely Nancy	18
Al Day's Waltz	19
Al's Minor	20
Always Loved Never Forgotten	21
Archie Minor	22
Auntie Ada's Waltz	23
Battle of the Somme	24
The Bees Knees Hop Step	26
Bonjour Mazurka	28
Chocolate Rabbit	29
Commonwealth Hornpipe	30
Commonwealth Jig	31
Coquetterie	32
Croissants et Café	34
David Stanton Waltz	35
Fairy Dance	38
The Flo Waltz	40
French Set – Rondeau	42
French Set – Bourrée	43
Fubu Waltz (version 1)	44
Fubu Waltz (version 2)	46
Gatwick Express	48
Glastonbury Hornpipe	49
The Green Shoots of Spring	50

The Harbour Inn Jig	51
The Hollesley Frolic	52
I Only Want to Dance with You	53
In the Toyshop	54
Jean's Waltz	55
Jenny's Hornpipe	56
King Cotton (Second Part)	57
La Marianne Waltz	58
Limey Pete	59
Little Eavie	60
Little Mark's Tune	62
Manor Royal March	63
Manor Royal Waltz	64
March of the Concertinas	66
Mazurka Gasconne	68
Mazurka Lapleau	69
Moonlight Hop	70
Morris Oxford	72
New Year Stomp	73
Oats and Beans	74
The Old Smithy	75
Old Tom Cat Hopstep	76
Pint of Cockles	78
Plasir d'Amour	79
Plum Duff	80
Processional March	82
The Queen's Jubilee	84
Ro's Tune	85
Shingle Street	86
Sidmouth Polka	87
Snow Flakes are Falling	88
Son Ar Chistr	90

Spring Bumbles	91
Stream to River Flows	92
The Day Thou Gavest, Lord, Is Ended	93
Three-Part French Schottische	94
Tom Tolley's Hornpipe	96
Turn off the Gas Mantle	98
Up with the Sparrow's Fart	100
The Wiggle Woggle Jig	102
Notes on the Tunes	109

Introduction

Alan Day has been playing the Anglo concertina for over 50 years, but he is relatively unknown outside the UK. That's unfortunate since he is one of the top proponents of playing the Anglo concertina in the harmonic style as well as being the composer of many tunes in the traditional style.

In addition to playing, performing, making videos, and attending sessions, he was also the prime instigator for two wonderful 3-CD sets of concertina music: *Anglo International!* (Folk Sound Records, 2005) and *English International!* (Folk Sound Records, 2008).

Initially learning to play the Anglo concertina as a member of Broadwood Morris, he was a co-founder of influential band Rosbif playing French traditional music, and he was also part of the George Inn Giant Ceilidh Band (GIGCB).

Alan has composed well over 60 tunes for the concertina, beginning with Auntie Ada's Waltz many years ago, and continuing up to the present. Forty-six of the tunes in this book are Alan's own compositions.

Most of the personal names in tune titles are friends and relations, some still alive and some sadly not. Alan likes to take these tunes to sessions, almost like taking these folks along with him.

He plays in a full-chorded style, and often employs the lower notes for a richer sound, and also for intricate walkdowns that greatly enhance the accompaniments.

> *I love the way Alan plays the concertina for the very reasons that make transcribing his music frustratingly difficult. He plays in a way that clearly is not bound to a paper version of the music. He plays what he hears, what he feels. He is free with ornamentation and never plays anything quite the same way twice.*
>
> David Barnert

Most of the tunes in this book have scannable QR code links to videos of Alan playing the tunes. He plays Jeffries Anglos in the keys of C/G and G/D, and some of the tunes he plays on both instruments. All of the tunes in this book are notated for C/G instruments since it is the most common, but the button numbers, bellows directions, and patterns will be identical for those who choose to play Anglos in other keys like G/D, Bb/F, etc.

Since Alan plays 39-button Jeffries concertinas, he has different accidentals on the upper right row as well as more alternate buttons than are found on a standard 30-button instrument. Consequently, a few minor accommodations have had to be made in select circumstances, which will hopefully be relatively unnoticeable.

About 20 years ago, Alan put together a tutor for the 20-button Anglo concertina for a friend, and although it has since been available online in various formats, it can be found here on the website of the International Concertina Association (ICA). Just keep in mind that he uses a different button numbering system than the one used in this and other Rollston Press books.

The Anglo and Alan

It was inevitable that I became a musician with both of My Grandfathers having dance bands and My Mum and Dad both playing piano. My Grandad on my Mum's side bought me a Swanee Whistle and I played in his little band on stage at about seven years old.

At Junior School I played violin, on one made by my Grandad (Dad's Father), but at Senior school this did not continue sadly as the Music teacher being Welsh was obsessed with choirs. I did however sing at The Royal Albert Hall. I started work with Mullard Equipment as an Apprentice Tool maker and joined their Glen Miller type band playing trumpet. (learnt at the Boys Brigade).

My love of the concertina started when one day on a drive in the country we saw the "Broadwood Morris Men" at the" Fox Revived Pub" nr Newdigate in Surrey. I knew one of the dancers (Sam) and we joined them for the day and I started to go to other evenings with them. One of the musicians (Brian Blanchard Folk Singer) played the Anglo Concertina, so when I was asked to join Broadwood I decided on the lovely little instrument that packed away in a small leather box.

My first concertina was a Hohner CG and the first tune I learnt on it was Shepherds Hey. On about the third trip out with Broadwood, the musicians didn't turn up so I had to play solo, not good for the nerves. I purchased a Jones concertina that needed a lot of work, but eventually traded it in for a CG Jeffries from Crabb Concertinas that you will hear on many of my recordings.

I made such progress with the concertina that I was invited to join "The Biggest Trio in the World" (About six of us) an English Country Dance band. We are fairly successful playing at a number of Folk Festivals and were invited to play in Paris, which included The Ris Orangis Folk Festival. It was here we first heard French Traditional Dance music and decided then that we enjoyed it so much that we would try and play this type of music. At our next trip to Paris we decided to play a set of Bourées as a break from what they expected (English Traditional). No calling is required for the dances, they just get up and dance. The reaction was amazing and the sound was different to what they were used to and we got a fantastic response.

Mel Stevens made himself a set of French pipes and a Hurdy Gurdy. We found Richard Smith (Who was treasurer of the Hurdy Gurdy Society) and we formed the band Rosbif. With two heavy droned instruments in the band I had to change my style of playing. We learnt the dances and started to do French Dance Workshops. All this was fairly new to the UK Folk scene and we made two records which both sold out.

I regularly attended the session at "The George" nr London Bridge run by Chris Shaw and he decided to form a big band which consisted of some of the players at the session. GIGCB (George Inn Giant Ceilidh Band) was formed. Initially about fifteen of us, but eventually consisted of Three Saxophones, Trombone, Guitar and Bass guitar, Flute, Two Melodions. Two violins and Concertina. We mainly played a mixture French, English and Breton Dance Music but did include a Russian, Italian and our own compositions. We played in France, Germany and the UK. This band is still alive and kicking, with regular bookings in France. With so many in the band it rarely covered expenses, but it was great fun and many of the gigs I would have paid to attend. Which in most cases I did.

On a regular visit to Sidmouth Folk Festival, I went to a number of sessions and concerts and listened to concertina players on the Anglo playing various styles, Irish, English, Jazz , singing accompaniment etc and it got me thinking that it would be interesting to make a CD that featured all these variations and showed the versatility of the Anglo.

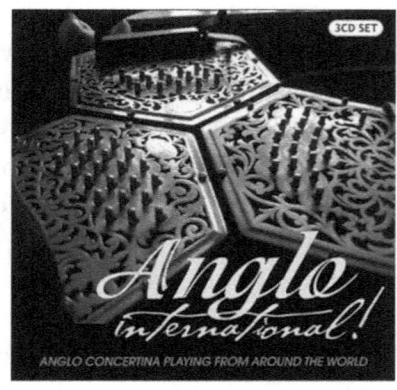

At a session I went over to John Kirkpatrick and discussed it with him and he agreed with me that it would be a really interesting project. I met him again about three years later and he asked me if there had been any progress, to which I said sadly no, but I promised him I would make a start. It took over two years to put the compilation together, contacting players World wide, gathering archive players, many players contacted me with recordings or to give me help and eventually Anglo International was born. With so many recordings of interest it became a three CD collection.

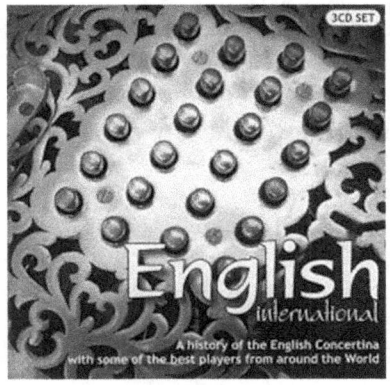

Anglo International received much acclaim and proved such a success that I was inundated with requests to follow it up with English International that again took about two years to put together a featured the World Champion Concertina Band of Ashton under Lyne and the runners up Harewood Concertina Band, both of whom are just fantastic to listen to. It also includes many archives of great players from the past and recordings of current players.

Duet International sadly did not happen, but Concertina.net agreed to host the recordings that have grown to a very comprehensive collection and not restricted to size, so viewing figures and Duet recordings are being added to on a regular basis.

I could not have achieved these compilations without a lot of help from players, sound recording specialists like Jim Ward and Wes Williams. and archives sent to me from all parts of the World.

All three collections have taken about seven years to compile, but well worth the effort.

Whilst living in Sussex I was invited to do an evening at the Elephant and Castle Folk Club. I really enjoyed the evening and got some nice comments at the end, including one from Mike Ainscough, a superb Jazz and folk guitarist. We decided to get together to see if we could combine our musical interests. I revived some of the music I was playing on the trumpet, with my other English, French Traditional music and Mike revived many of his favourites, including Music Hall songs. We had a great time and received a number of bookings that included The Underground Theatre at Eastbourne, where we played in front of a sell out at everyone we did.

We made a CD of our playing and we sold all of them. It was great fun with Mike and if I ever do the long trip from Suffolk to Sussex we shall renew our partnership.

I now play at regular sessions in Suffolk and the odd Folk Club, playing a mixture of the tunes from this book and a few old Music Hall songs and Monologues.

I must admit to be very honoured to be asked by Gary to do this book and I have enjoyed working with Gary, who has been very professional and a pleasure to work with.

ALAN DAY
February 2024

Keyboard & Tablature

The button numbering system used here for 30-button Anglo concertinas in the key of C/G:

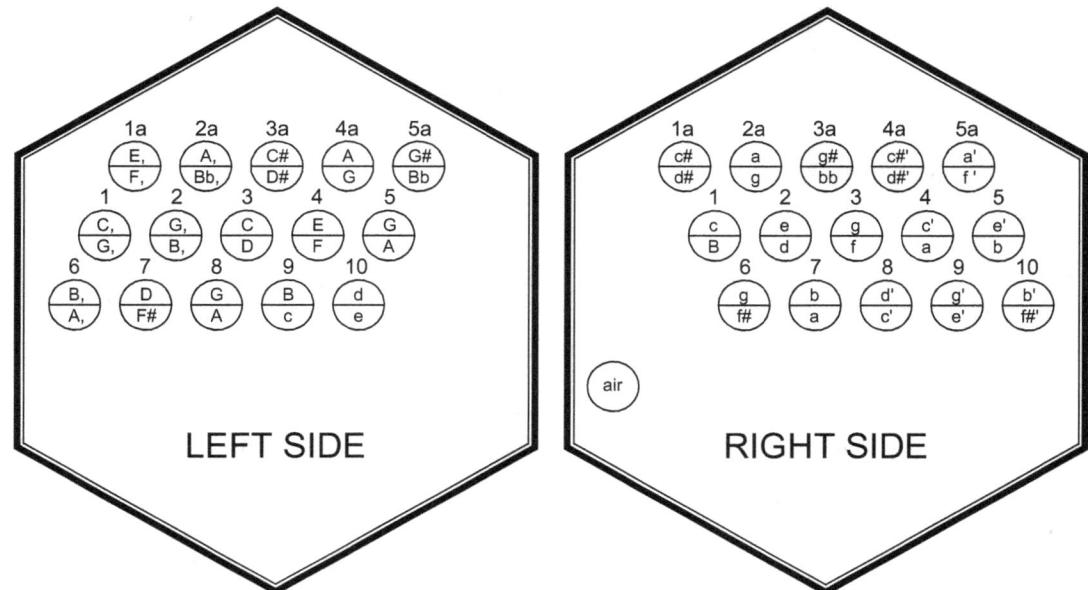

Low notes are on the left side of the instrument and high notes are on the right. Notes shown above the line are on the push, notes shown below the line are on the pull. Standard abc notation has been used to show the pitches of the notes.

How the tablature works in this book:

- The buttons are numbered using the "1a-10" numbering system for each side.
- Buttons on the right-hand side are shown above the musical notes.
- Buttons on the left-hand side are shown below the musical notes.
- Notes on the push are shown by button number only.
- Notes on the pull are shown by button number with a line across the top.
- Long phrases all on the pull will have one long continuous line above the button numbers.
- Notes that are held longer are indicated with dashed lines after the button number.

EXAMPLE:

Each tune also has a Button Map showing the buttons needed to play that particular tune:

Buttons played

14   The Anglo Concertina Music of Alan Day

The Old Concertina

The Abigail Waltz

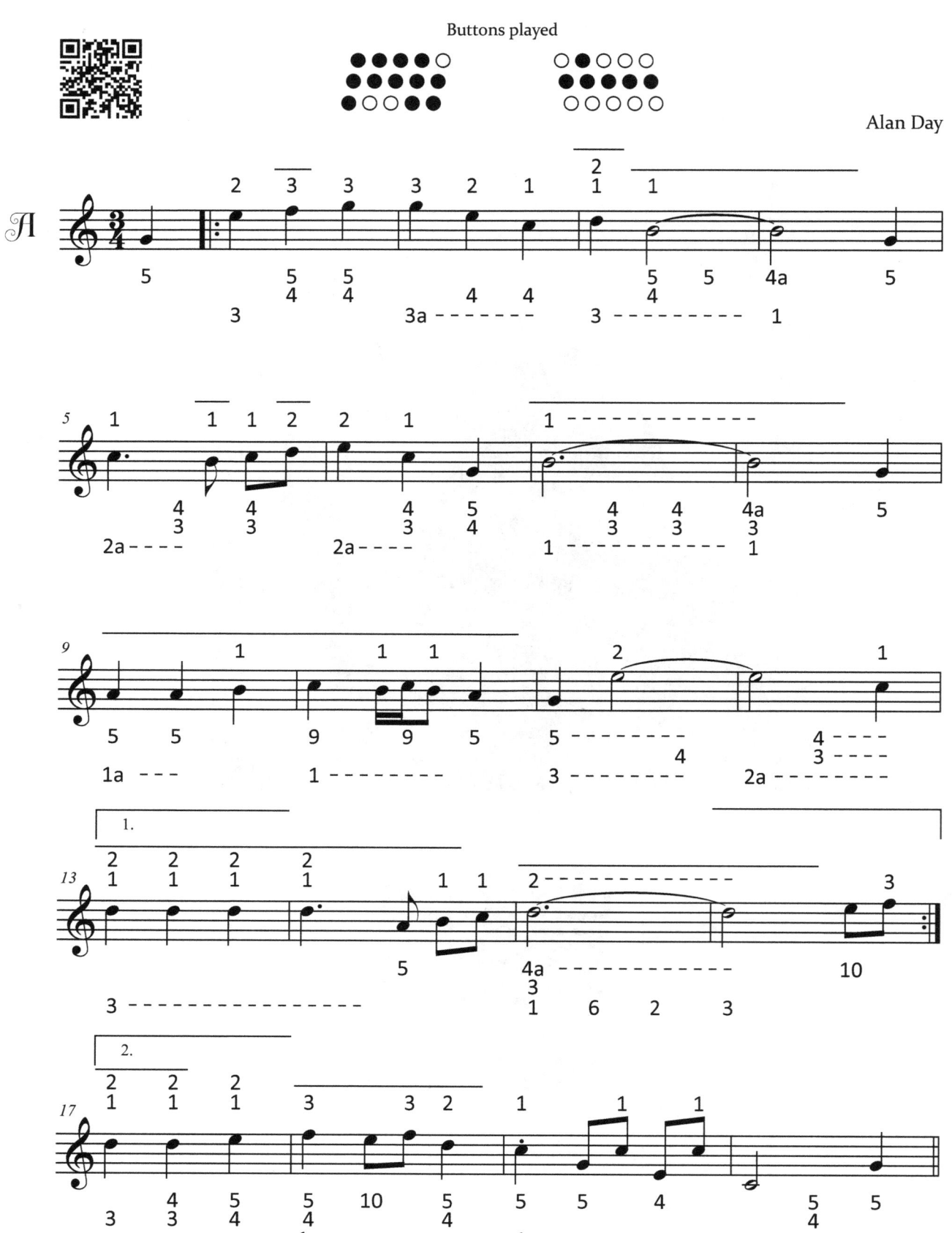

The Anglo Concertina Music of Alan Day

Adieu Sweet Lovely Nancy

Buttons played

Traditional

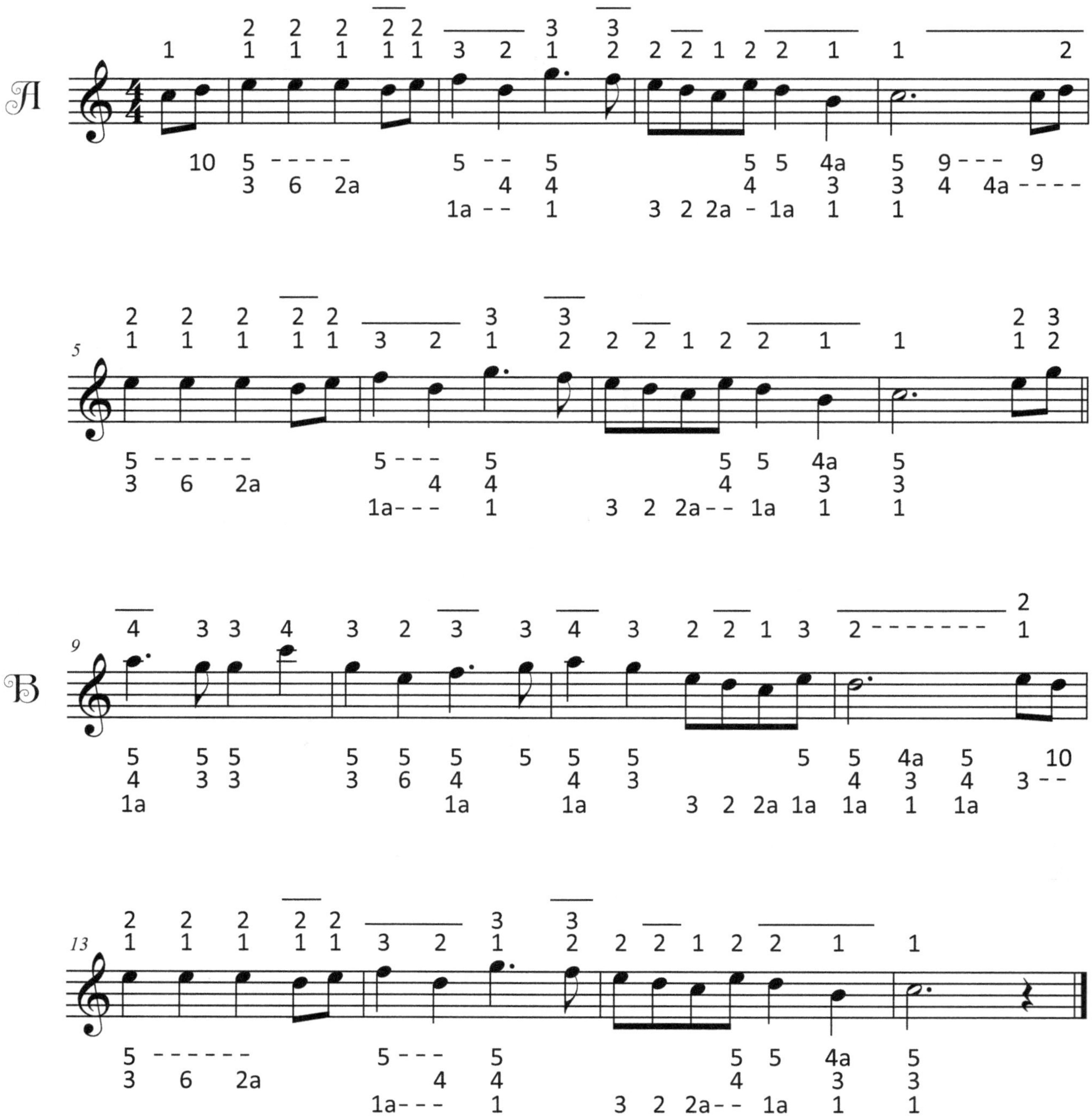

Al Day's Waltz

Buttons played

Alan Day

Al's Minor

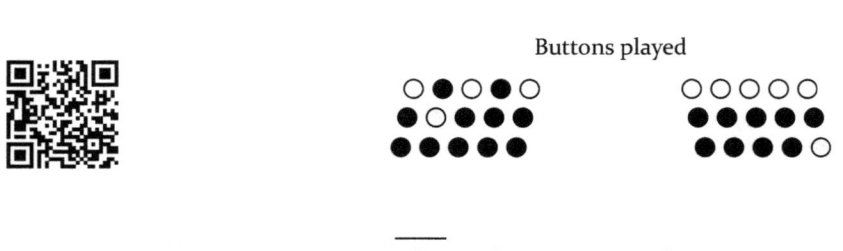

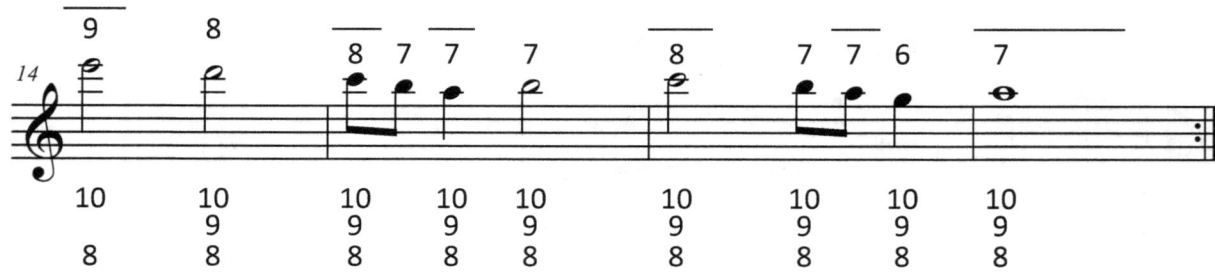

Always Loved Never Forgotten

Buttons played

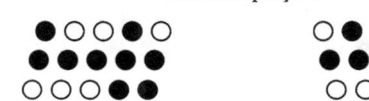
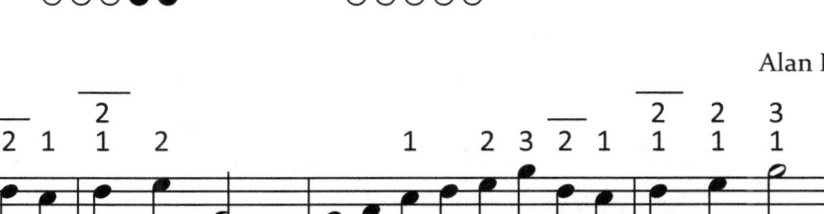

Alan Day

D.C. al Fine

Archie Minor

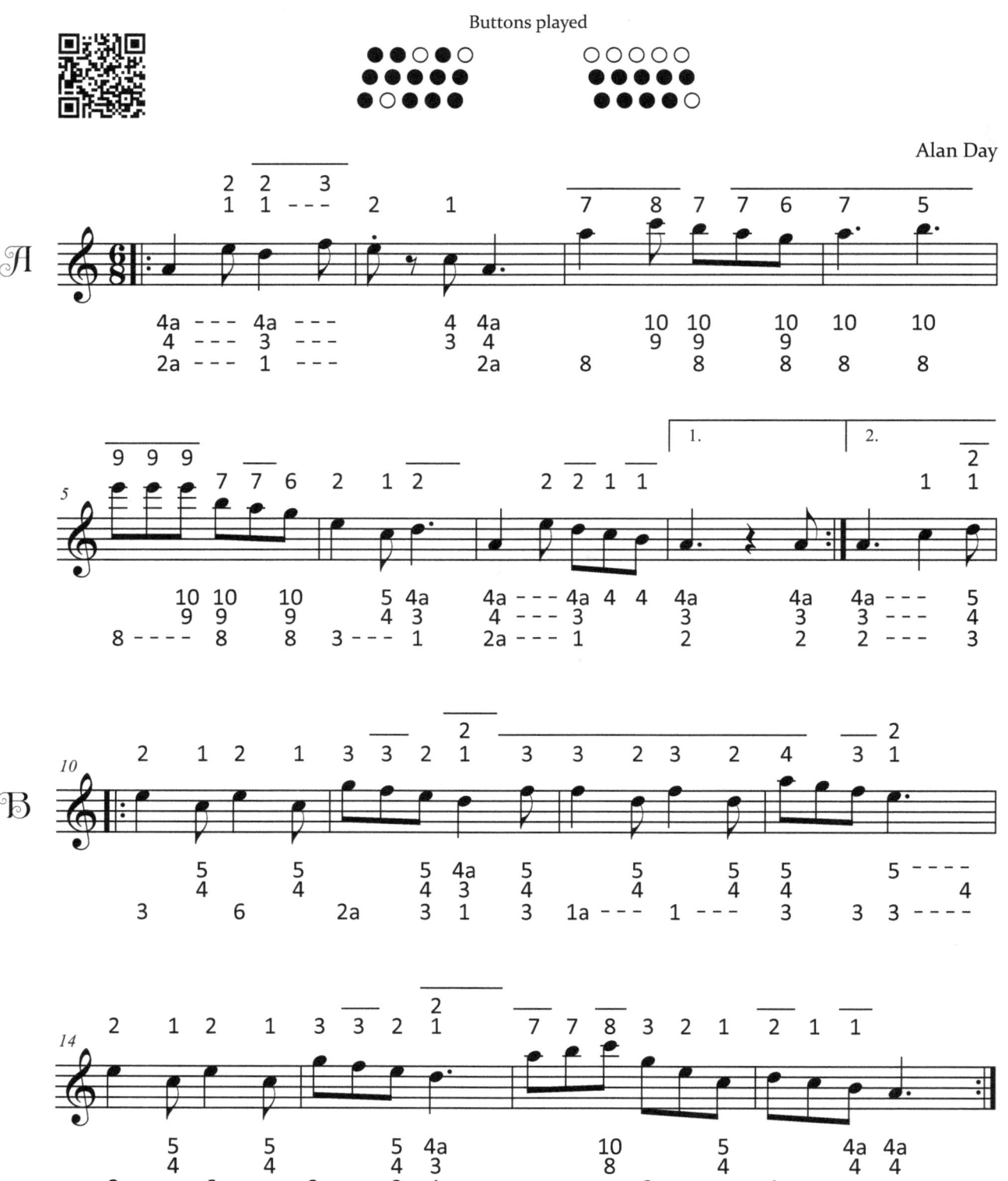

Auntie Ada's Waltz

NOTE: This tune has been transposed from the key of G to the key of C.

The Battle of the Somme

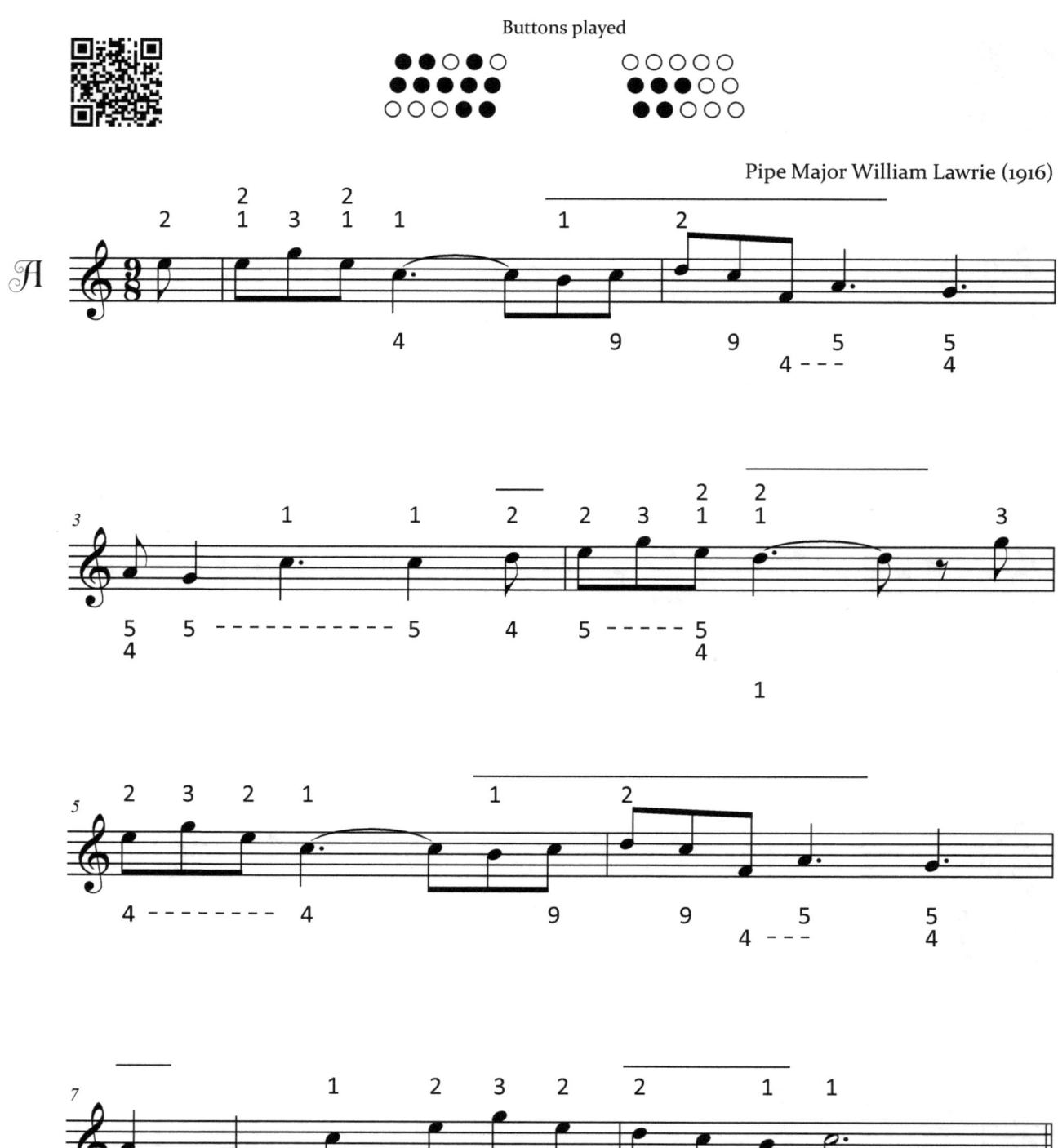

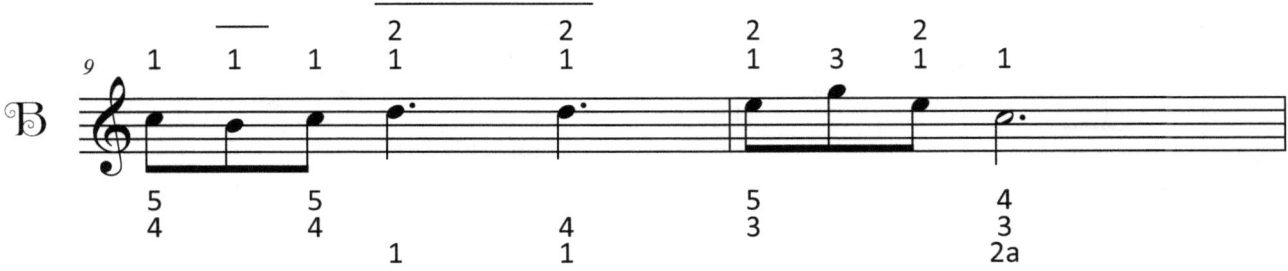
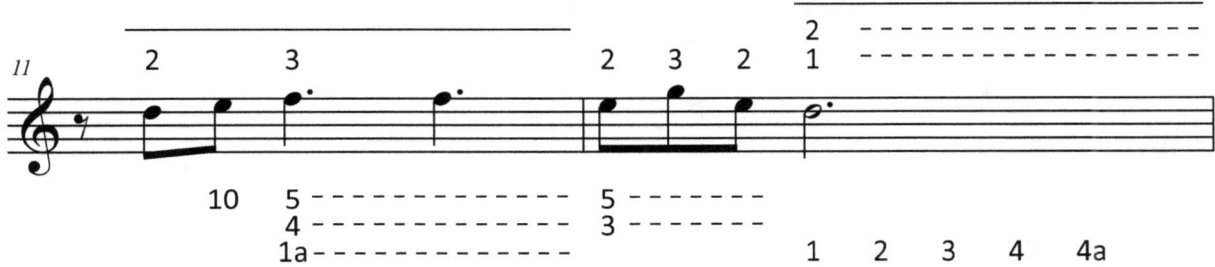
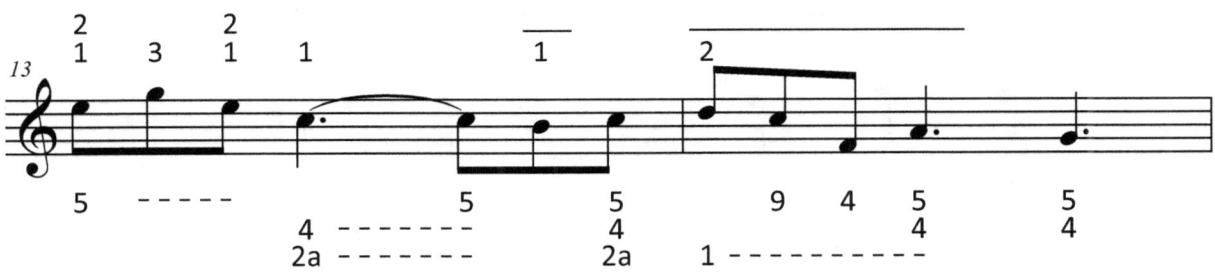

The Bees Knees Hop Step

Alan Day

Bonjour Mazurka

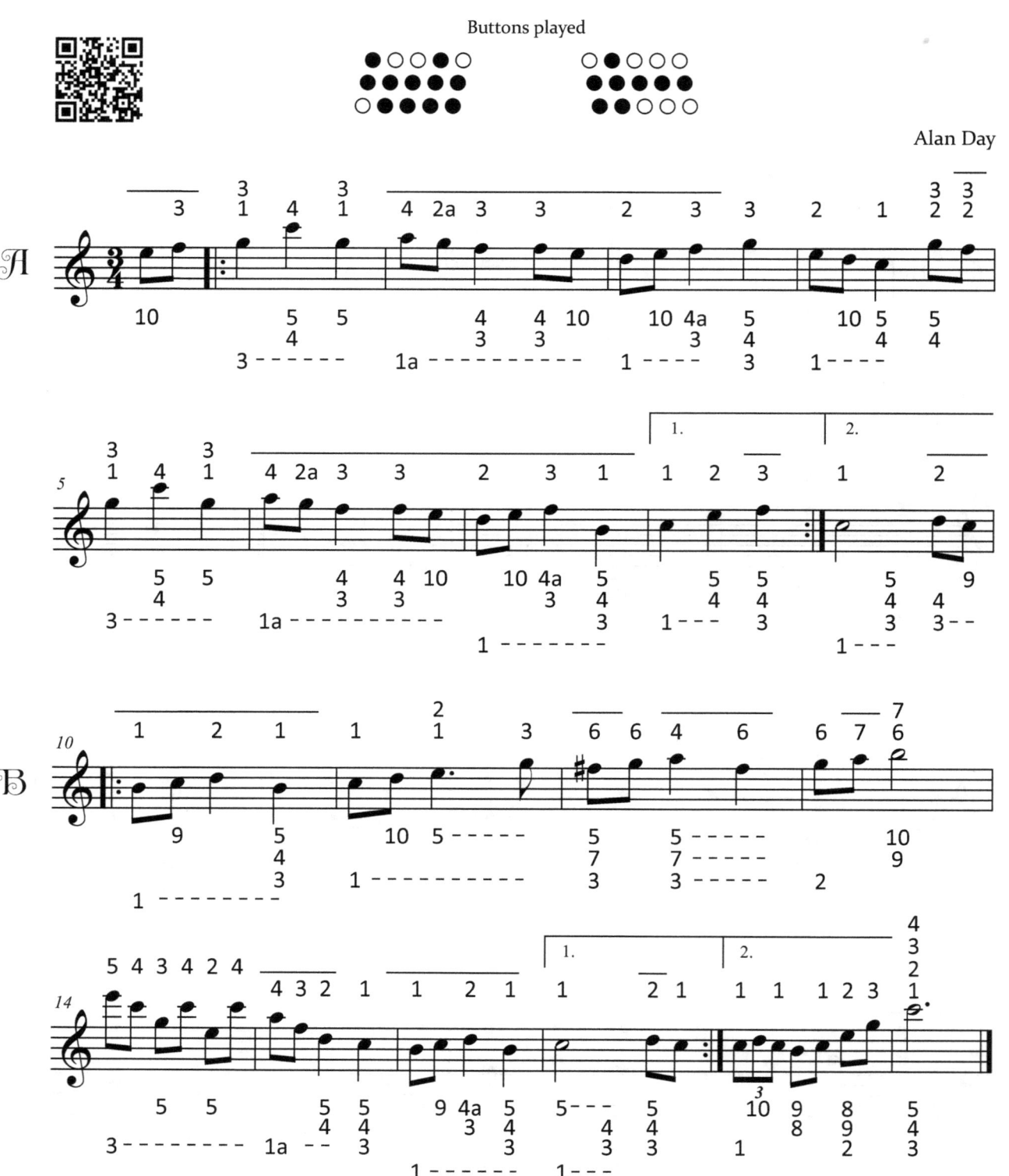

Chocolate Rabbit

Buttons played

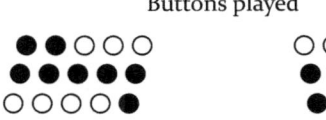

Alan Day

Commonwealth Hornpipe

Commonwealth Jig

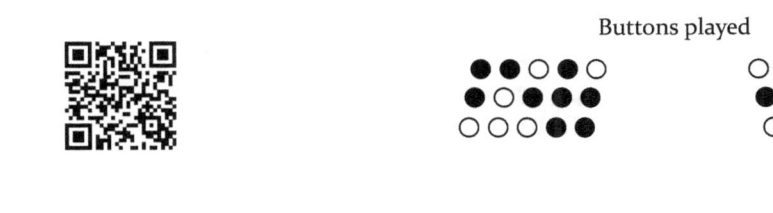

Alan Day

Coquetterie

Croissants et Café

Alan Day

The David Stanton Waltz

Alan Day

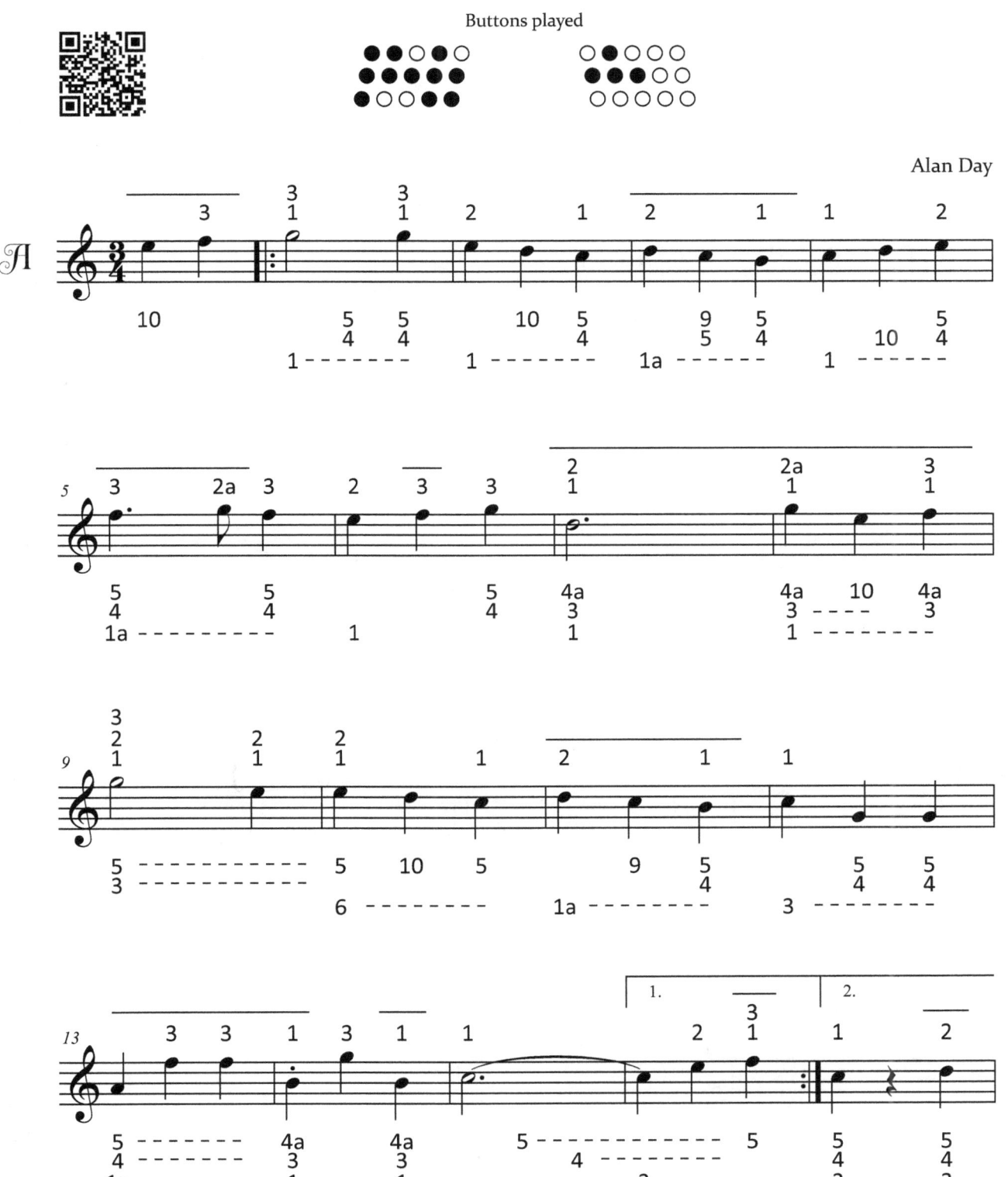

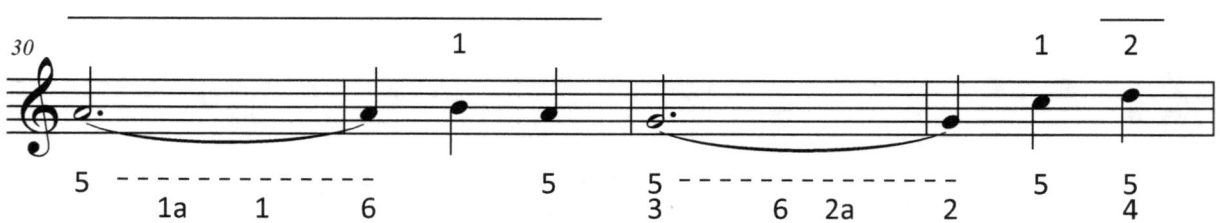

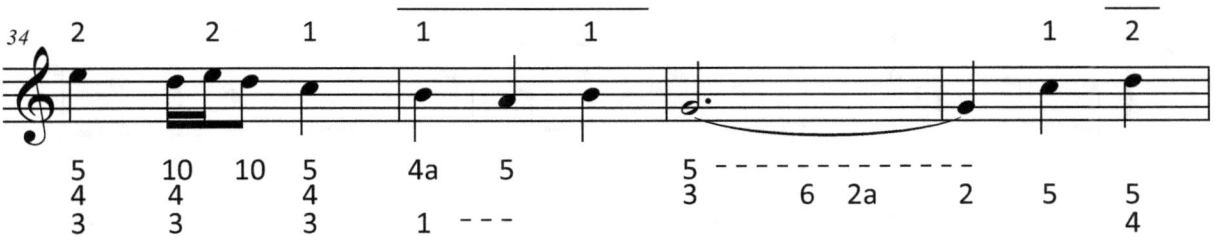

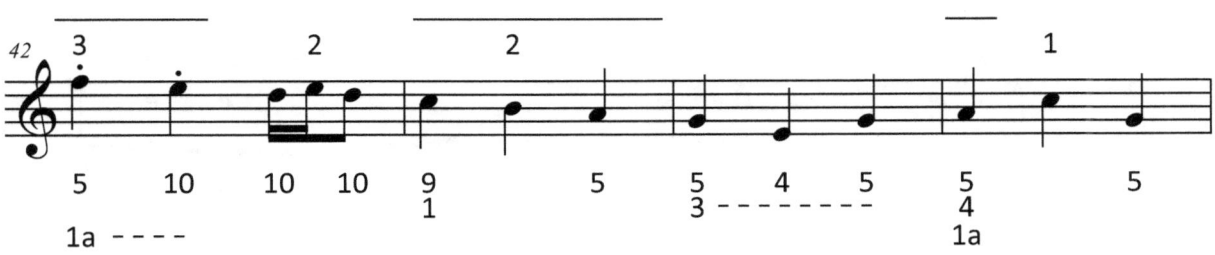
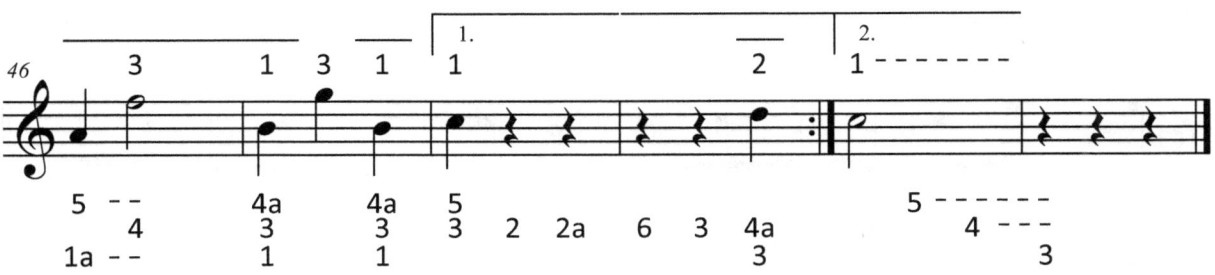

Fairy Dance

Buttons played

 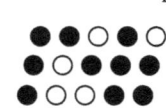 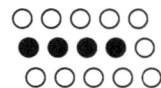 

Traditional

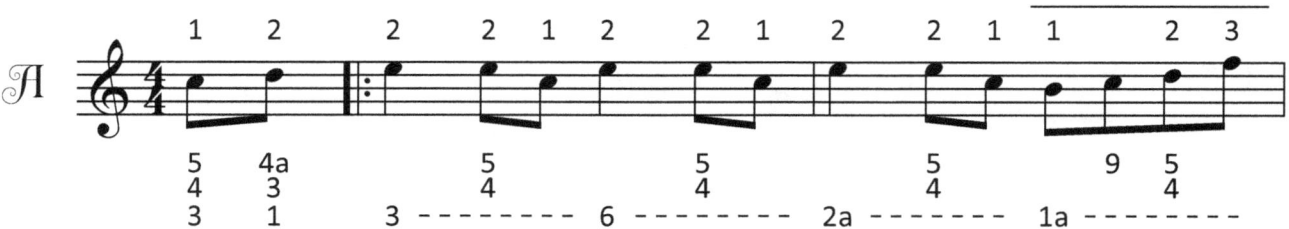

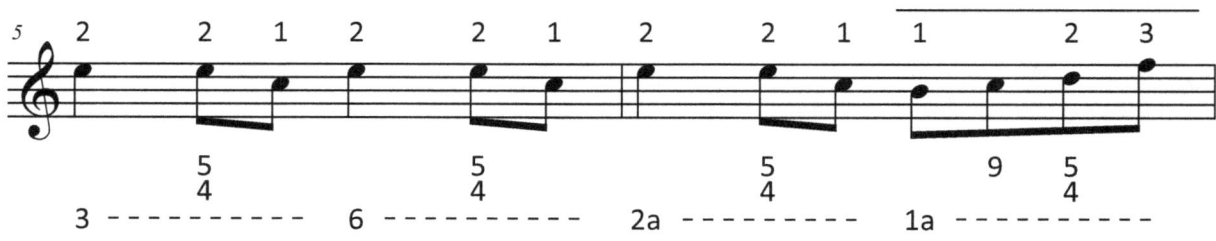

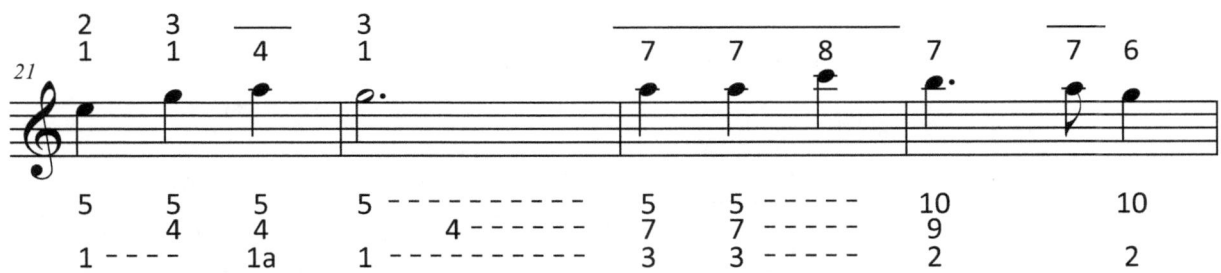
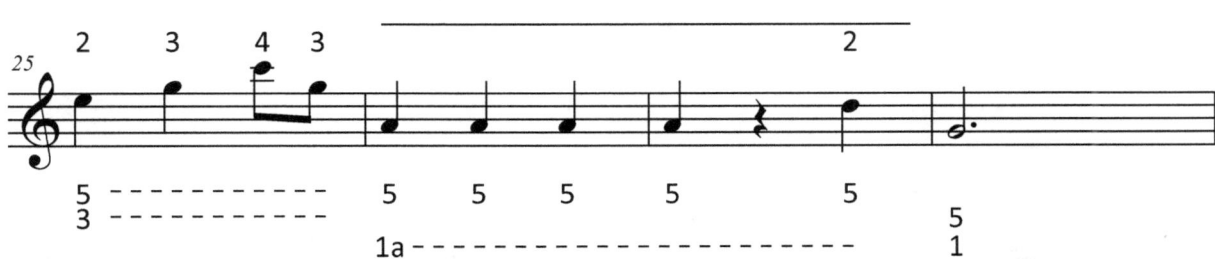

The Anglo Concertina Music of Alan Day

French Set - Rondeau

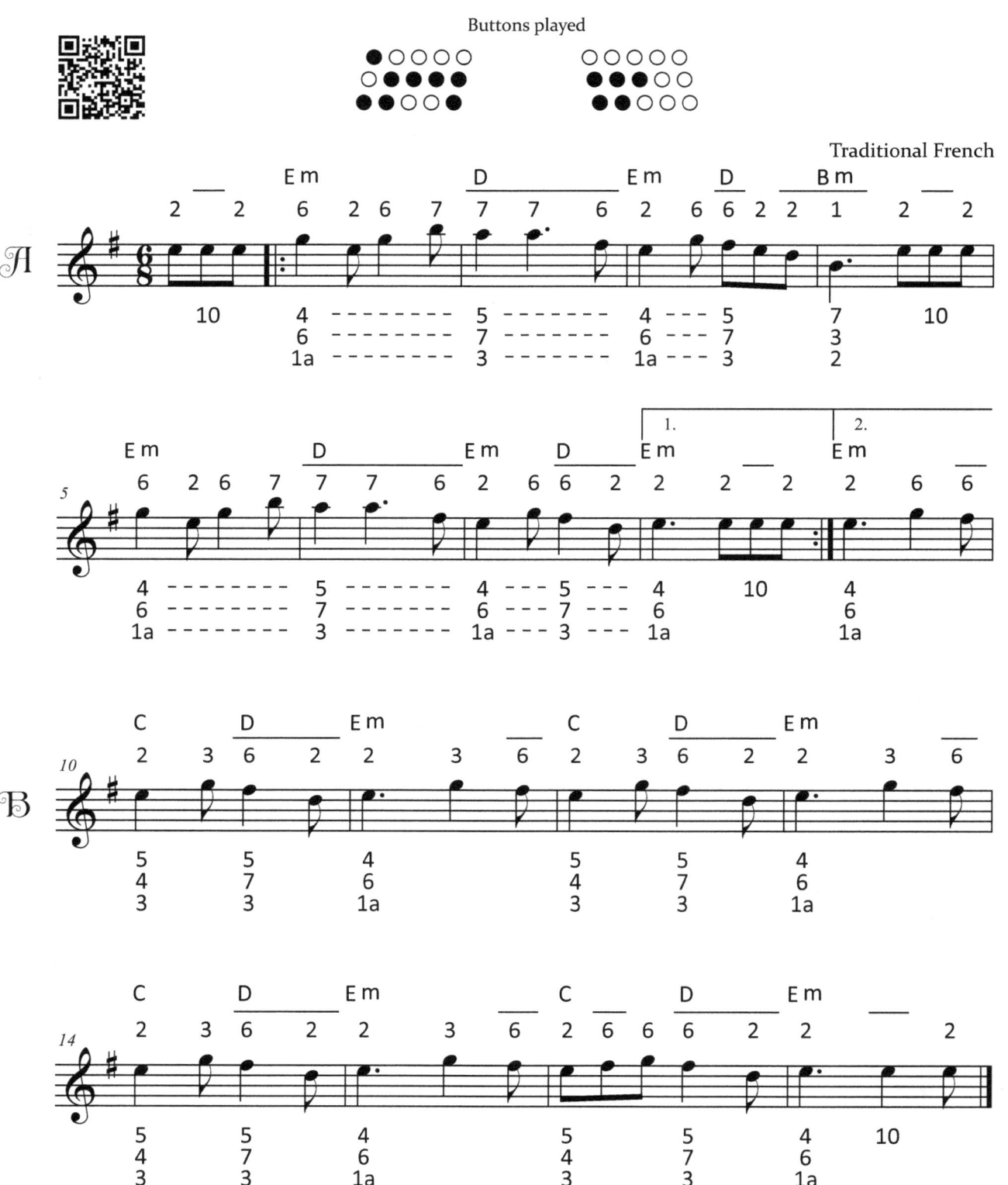

French Set - Bourrée

Buttons played

Traditional French

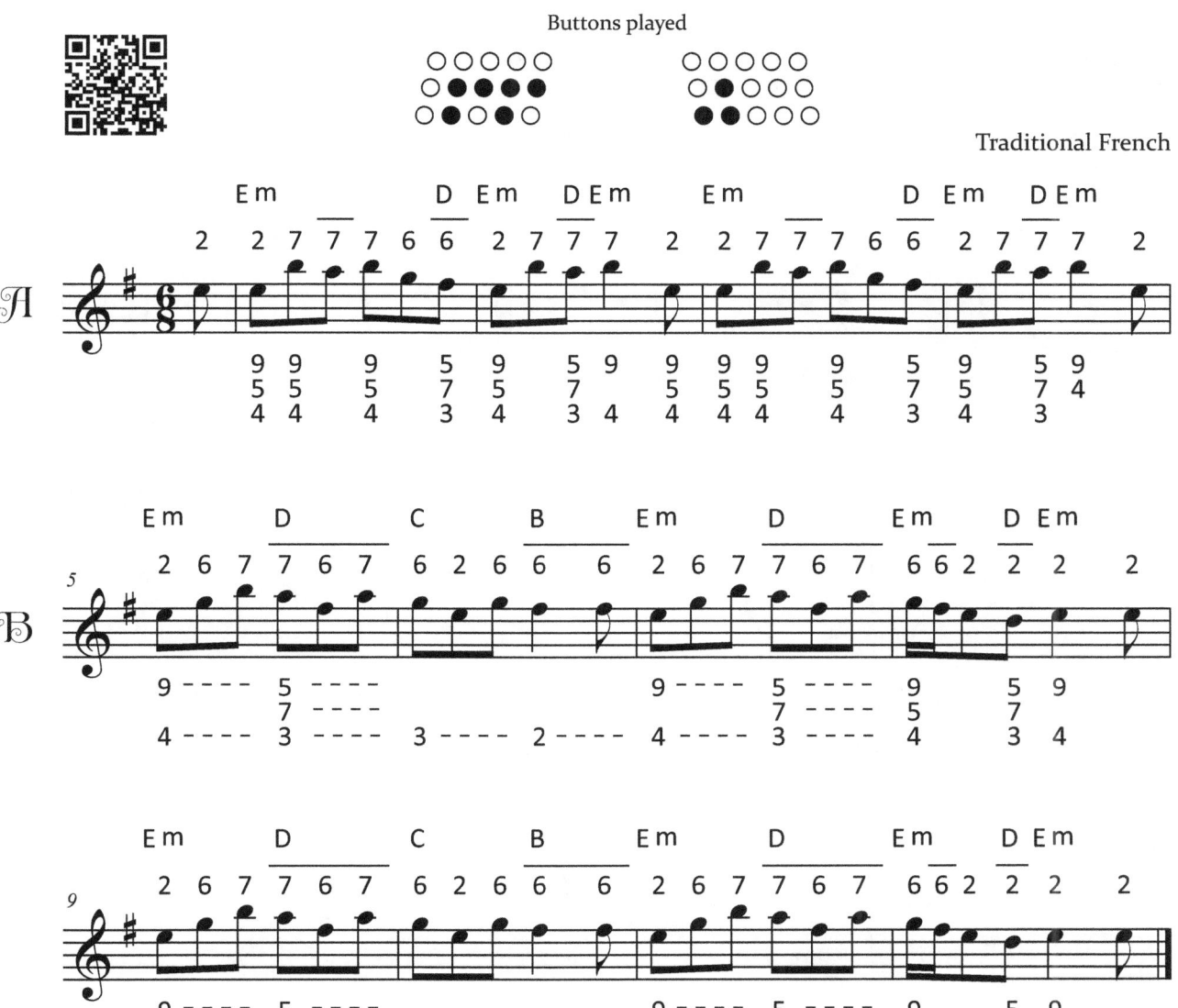

Fubu Waltz (Version 1)

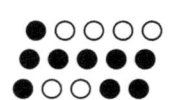
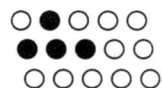

Buttons played

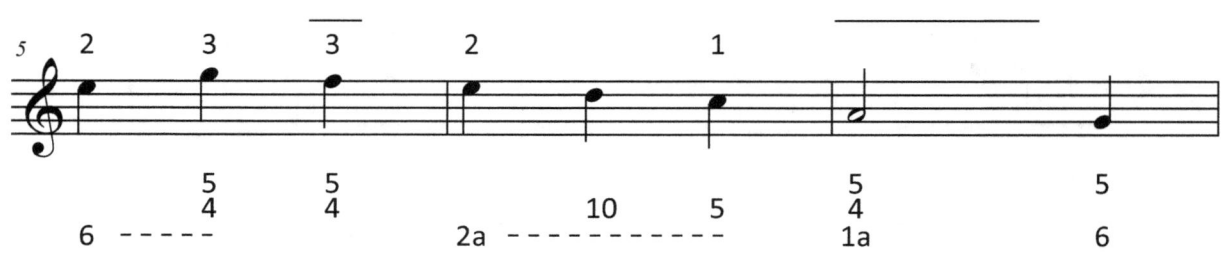

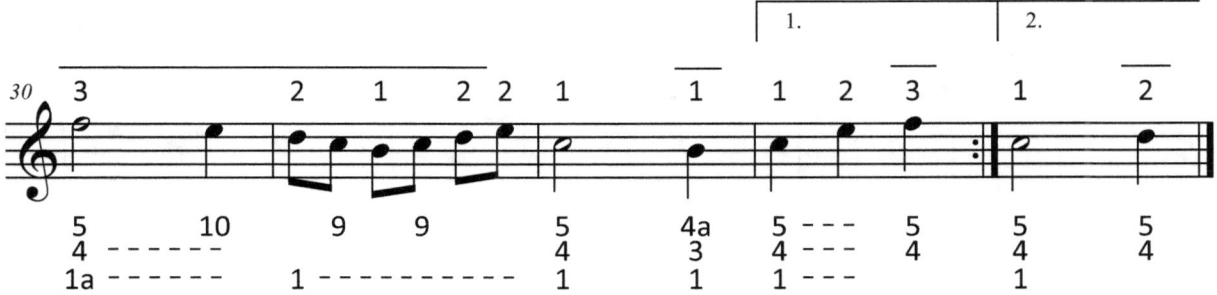

Fubu Waltz (Version 2)

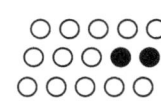
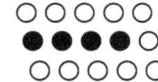

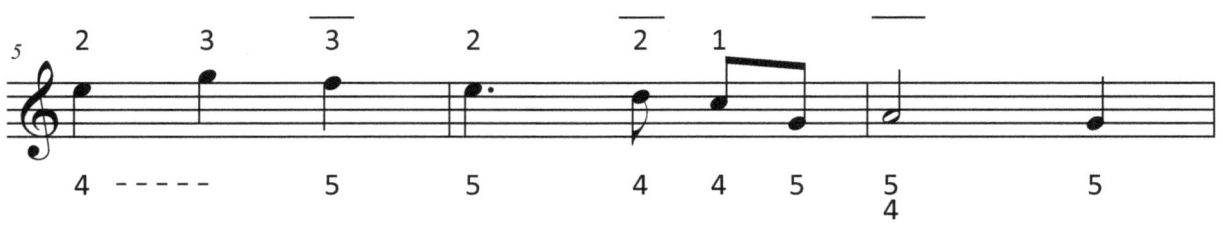

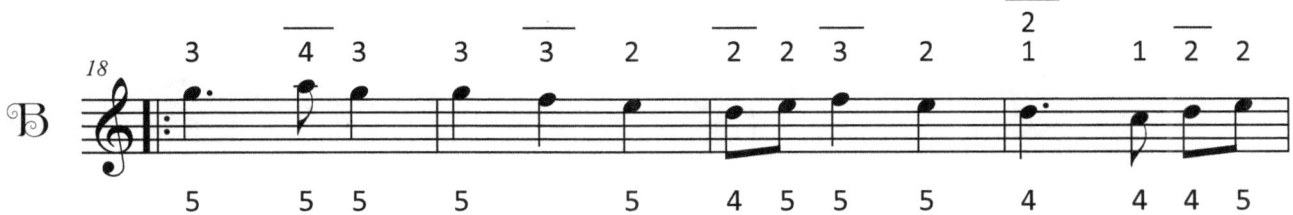

Gatwick Express

Buttons played

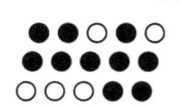
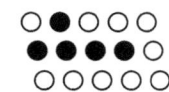

Alan Day

The Glastonbury Hornpipe

Alan Day

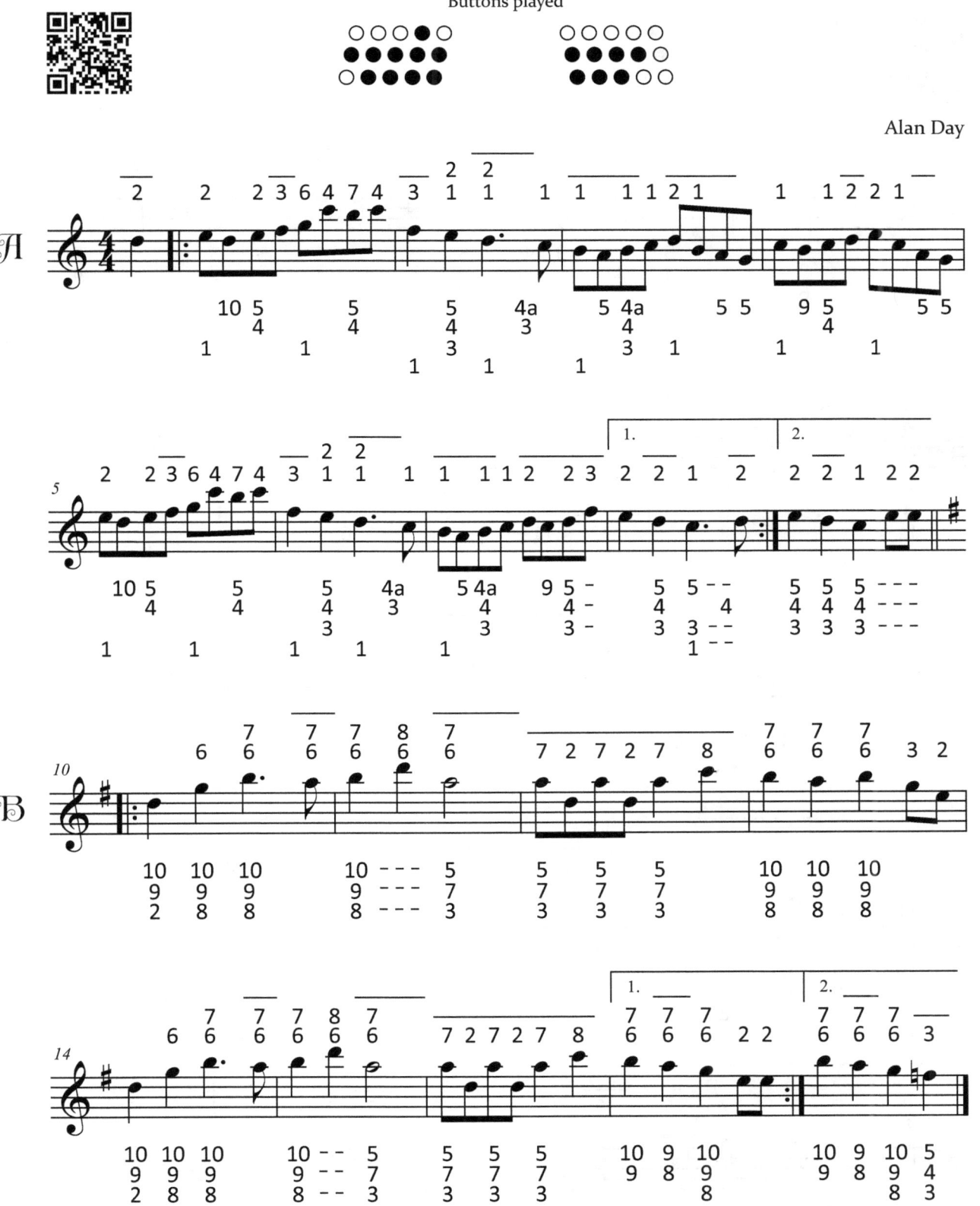

The Green Shoots of Spring

Alan Day

The Harbour Inn Jig

The Hollesley Frolic

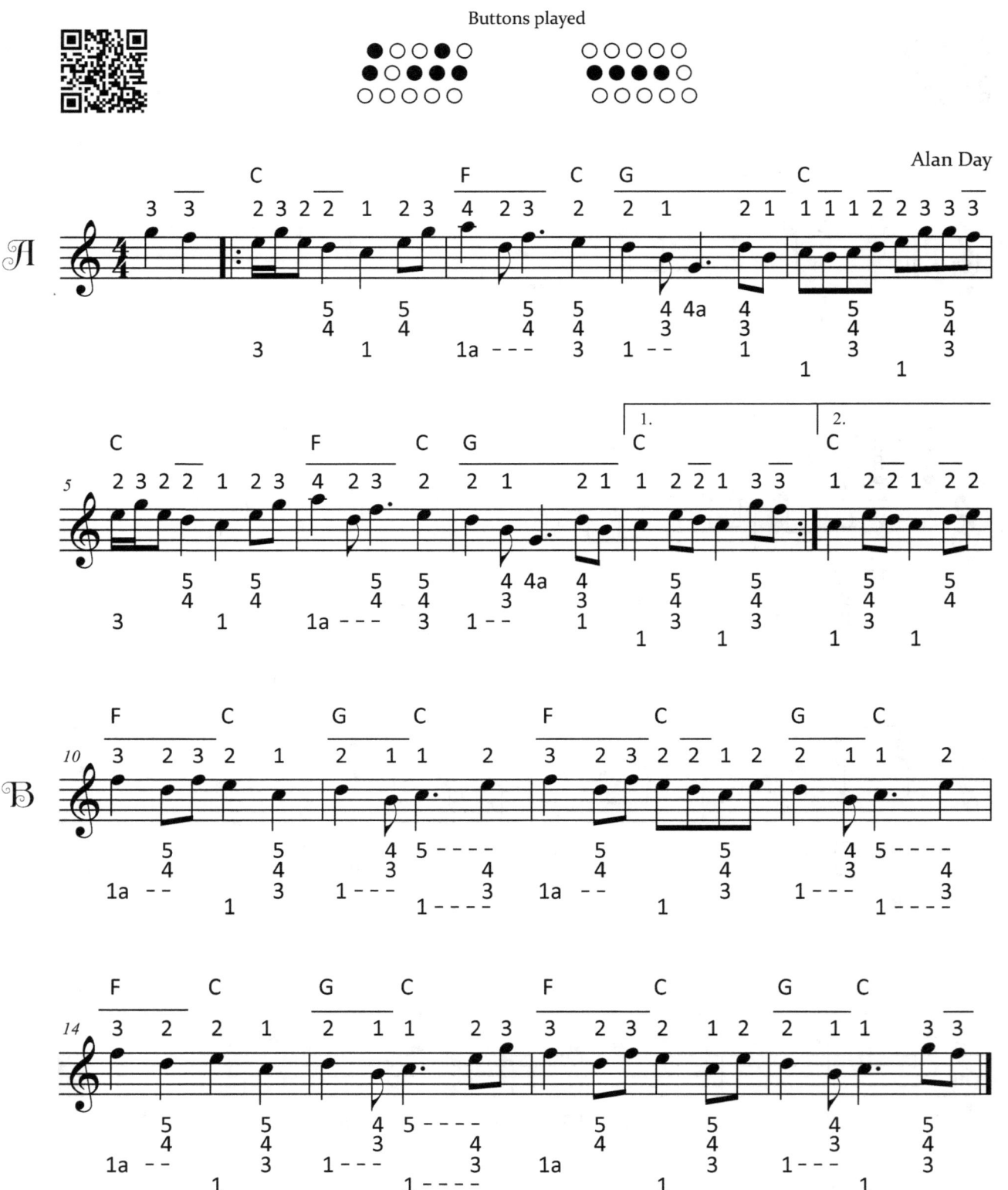

I Only Want to Dance with You

Buttons played

  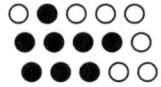

Alan Day

D.C. al Fine

In the Toyshop

Jean's Waltz

Jenny's Hornpipe

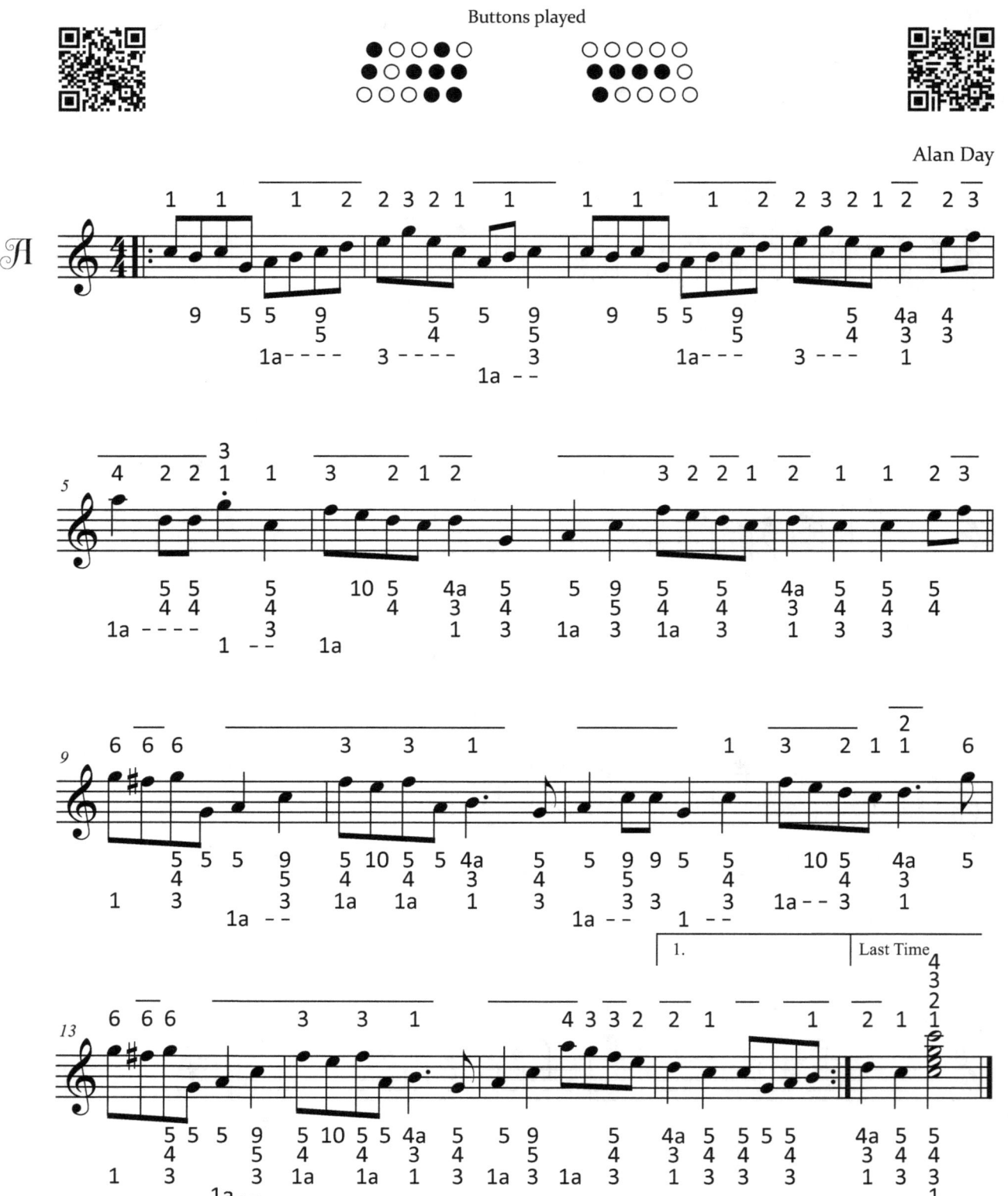

NOTE: Transposed from the key of G to the key of C.

King Cotton (2nd Part)

Buttons played

John Philip Sousa (1895)

La Marianne

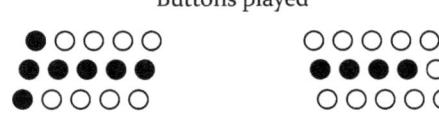

Traditional French

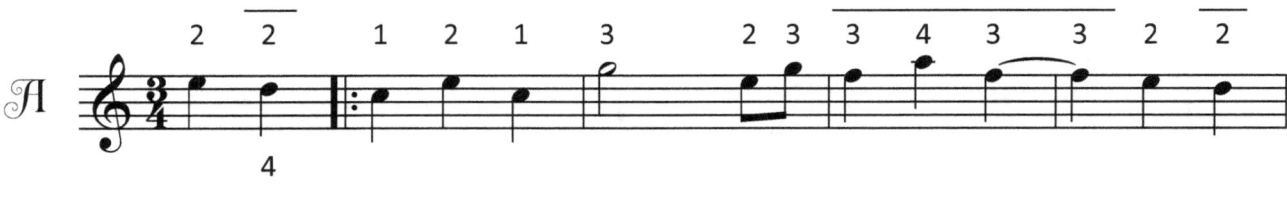
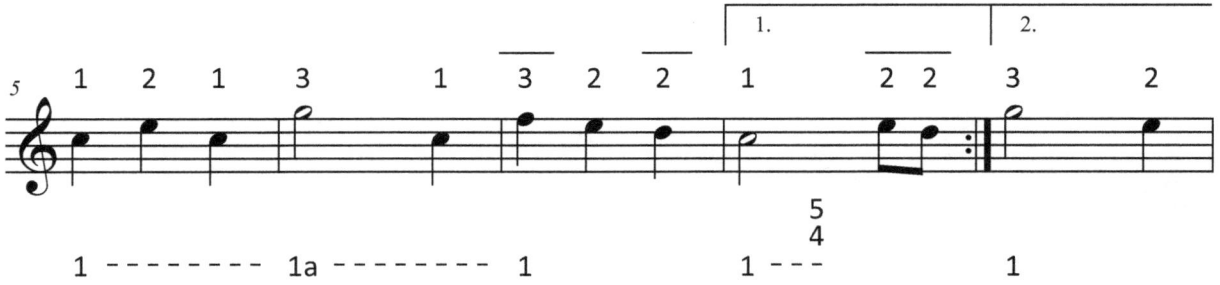

LIMEY PETE

Buttons played

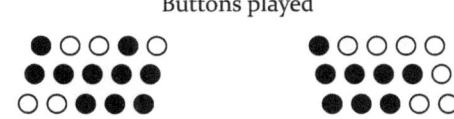

Alan Day

Little Eavie

Alan Day

Little Mark's Tune

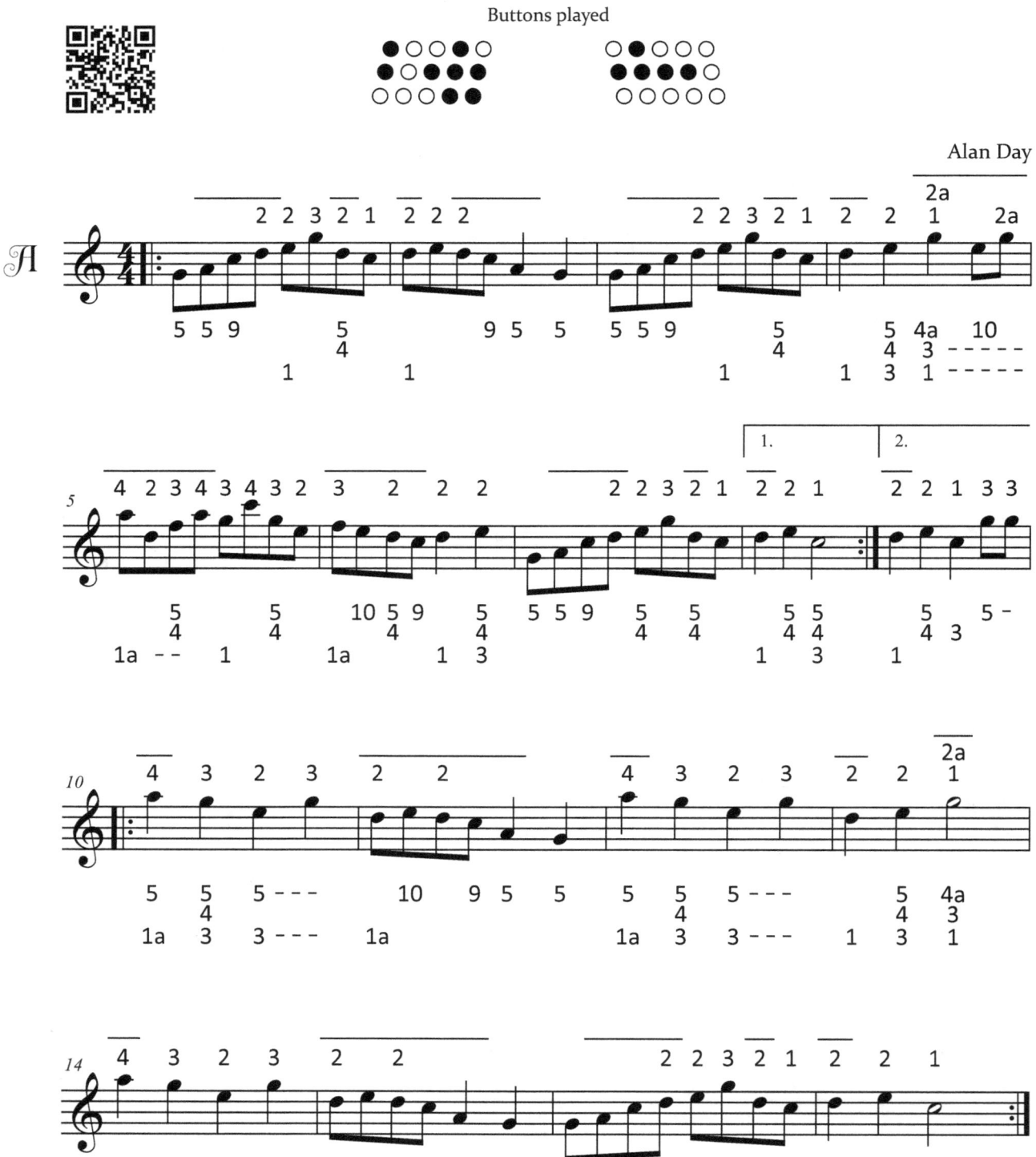

Manor Royal March

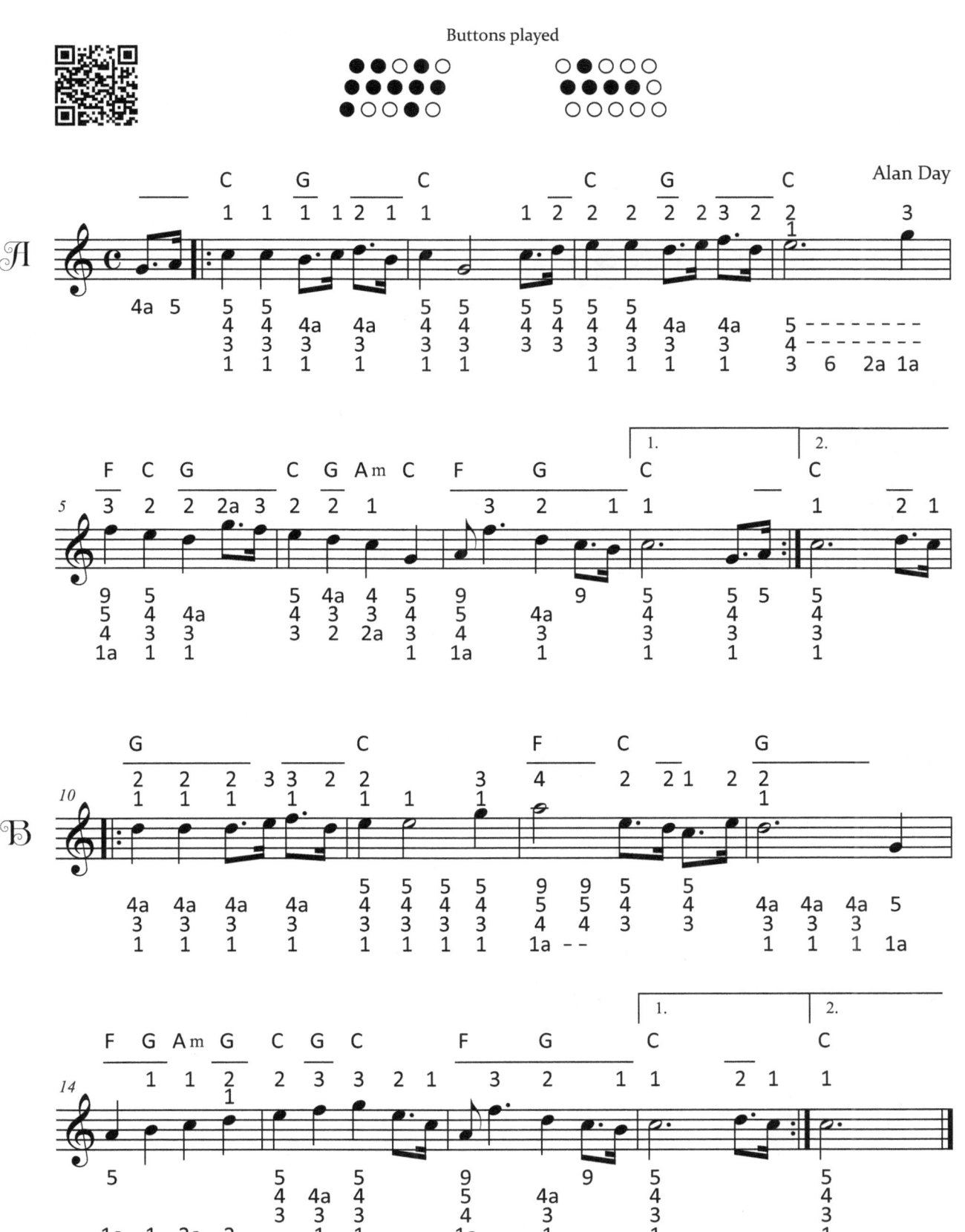

Manor Royal Waltz

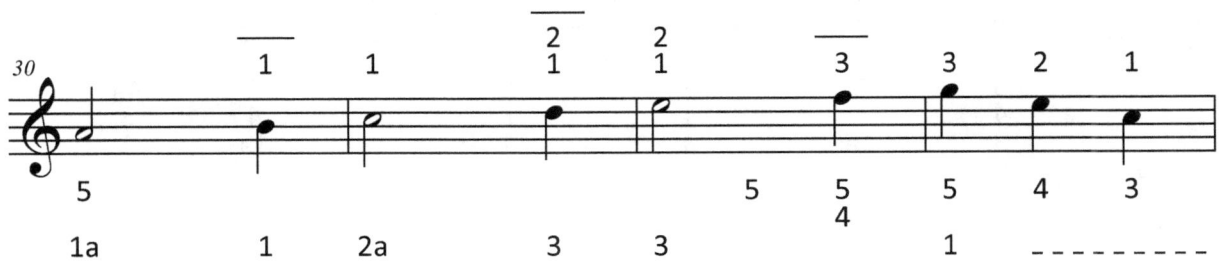

The Anglo Concertina Music of Alan Day

March of the Concertinas

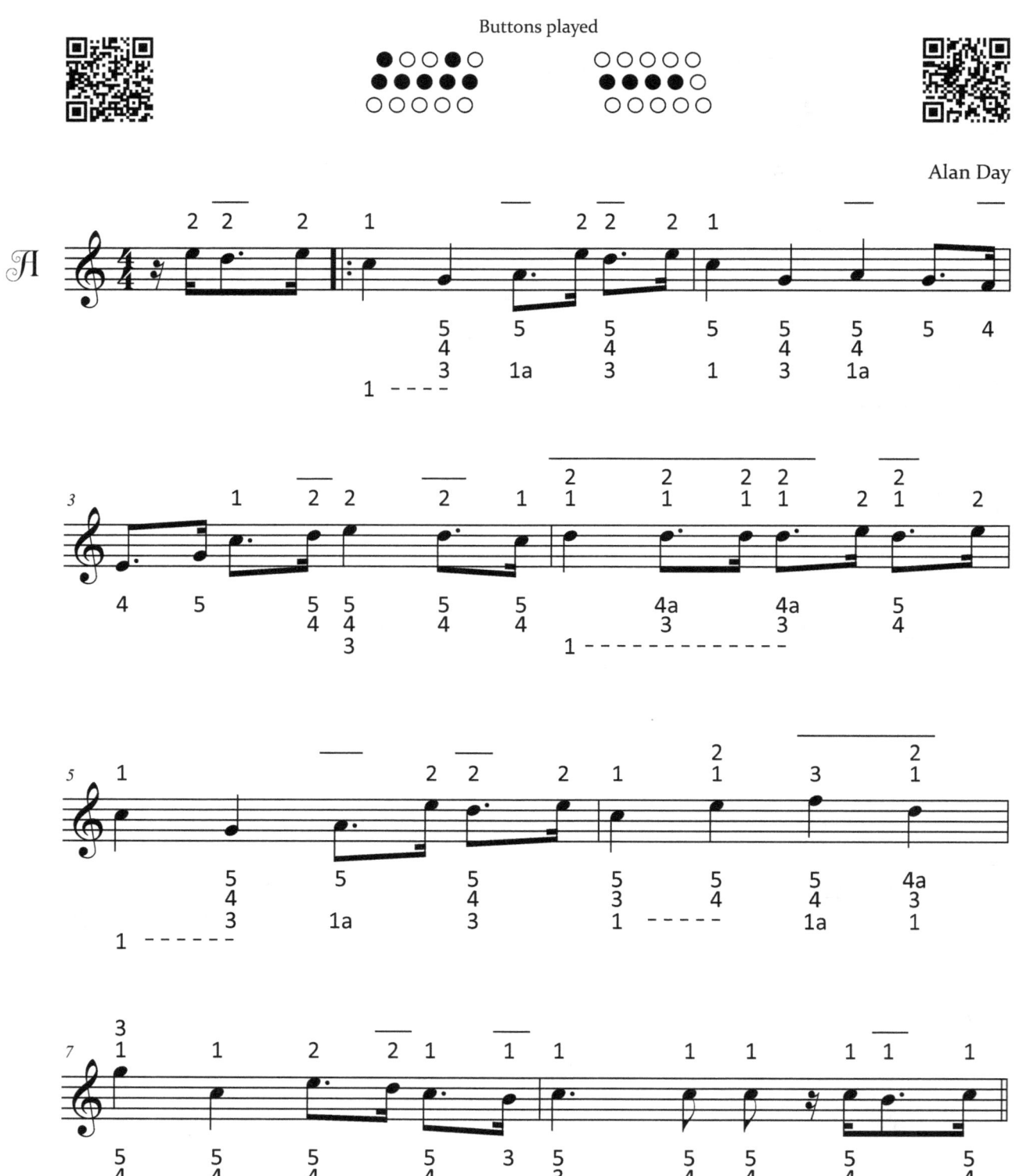

Mazurka Gasconne

Mazurka Lapleau

Buttons played

Traditional French

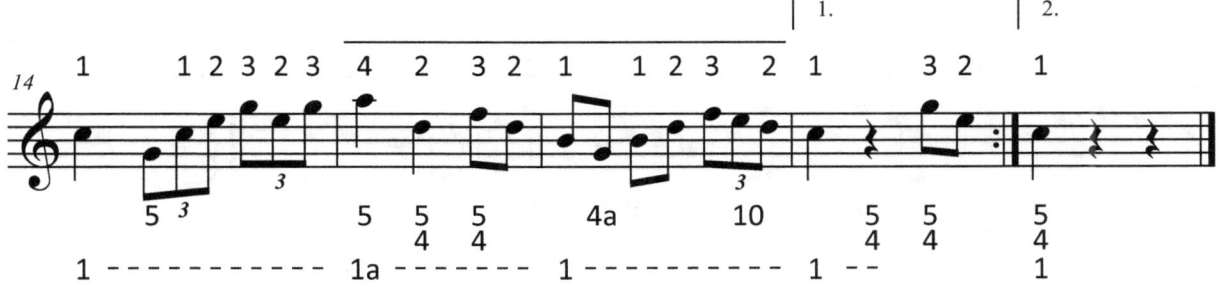

Moonlight Hop

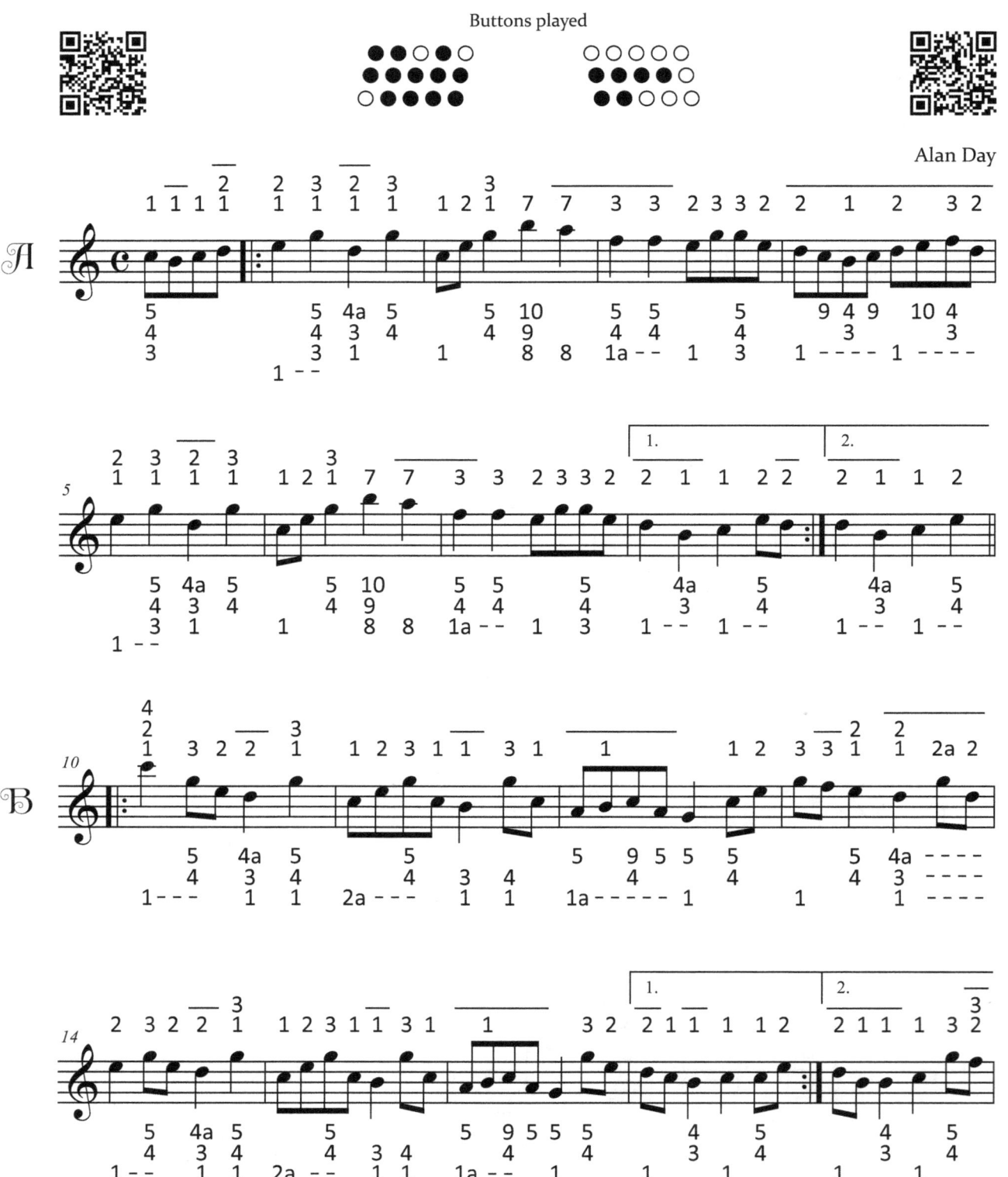

Morris Oxford

New Year Stomp

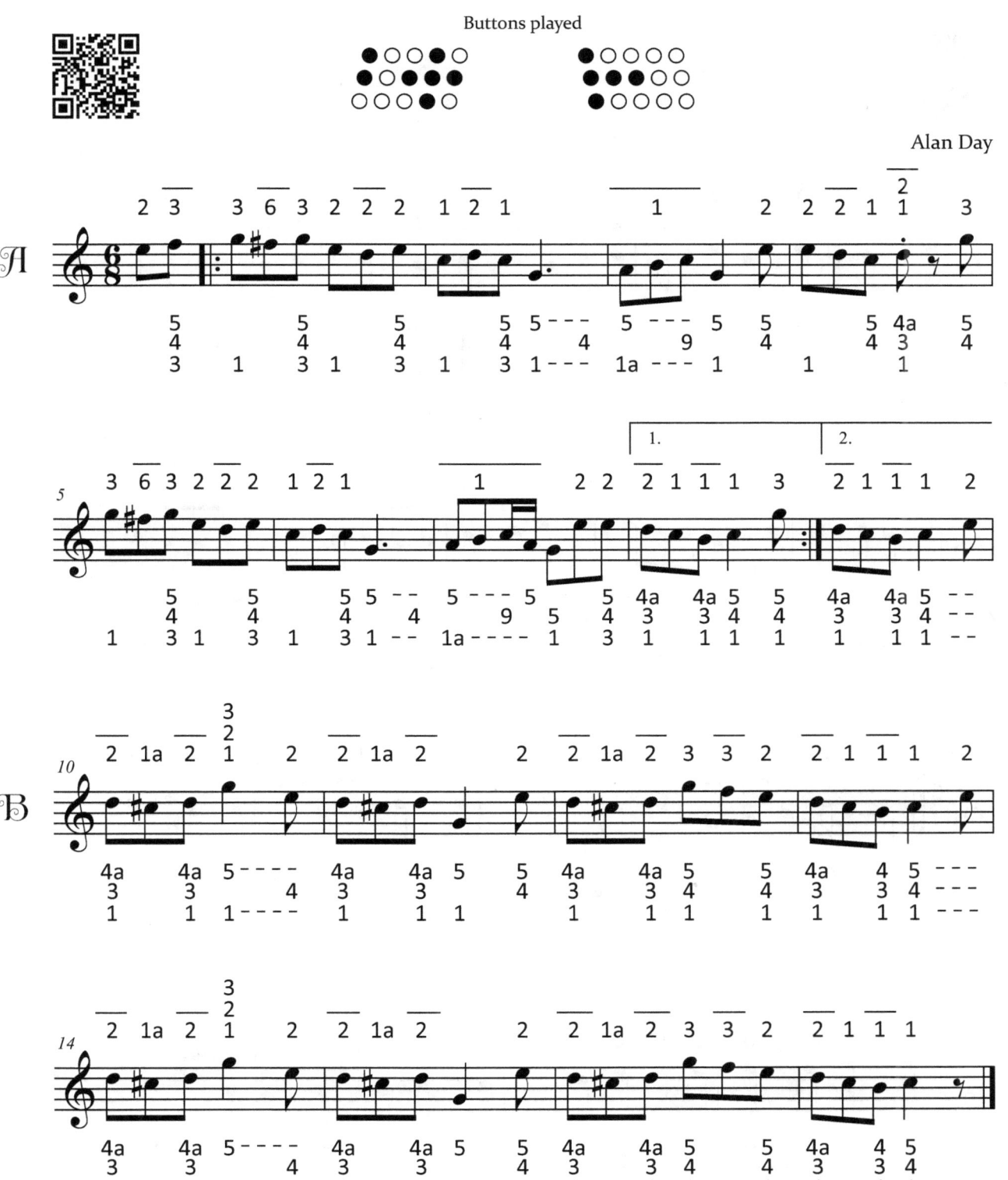

OATS AND BEANS

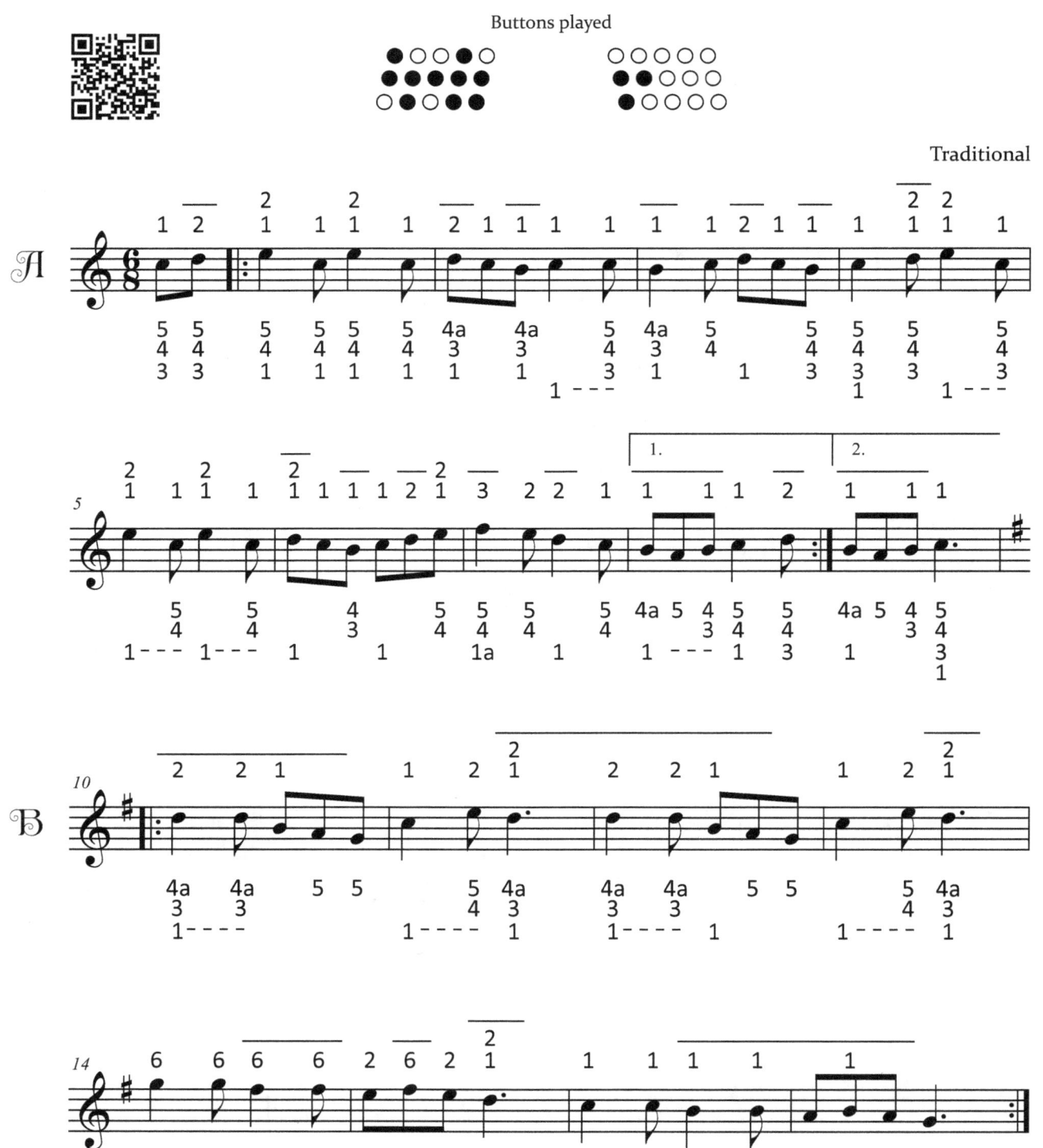

The Old Smithy

The Old Tom Cat Hopstep

Buttons played

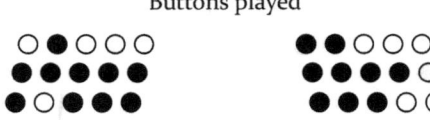

Alan Day

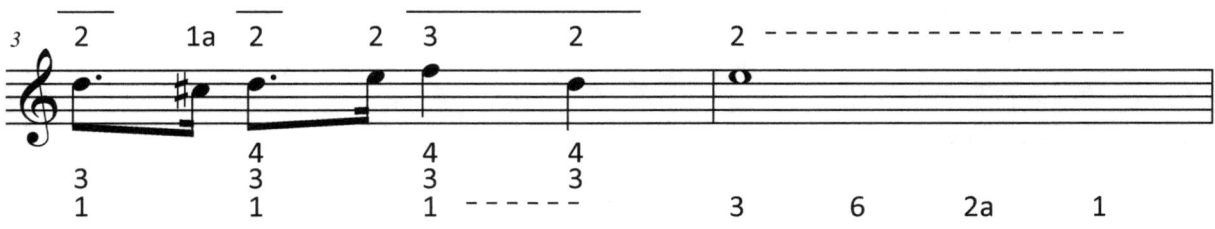

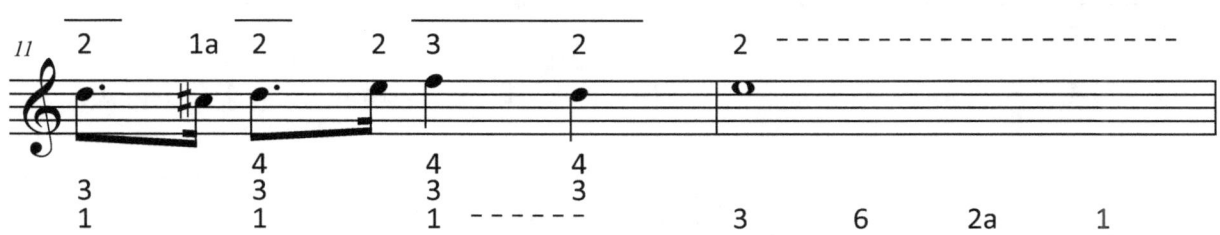

Pint of Cockles

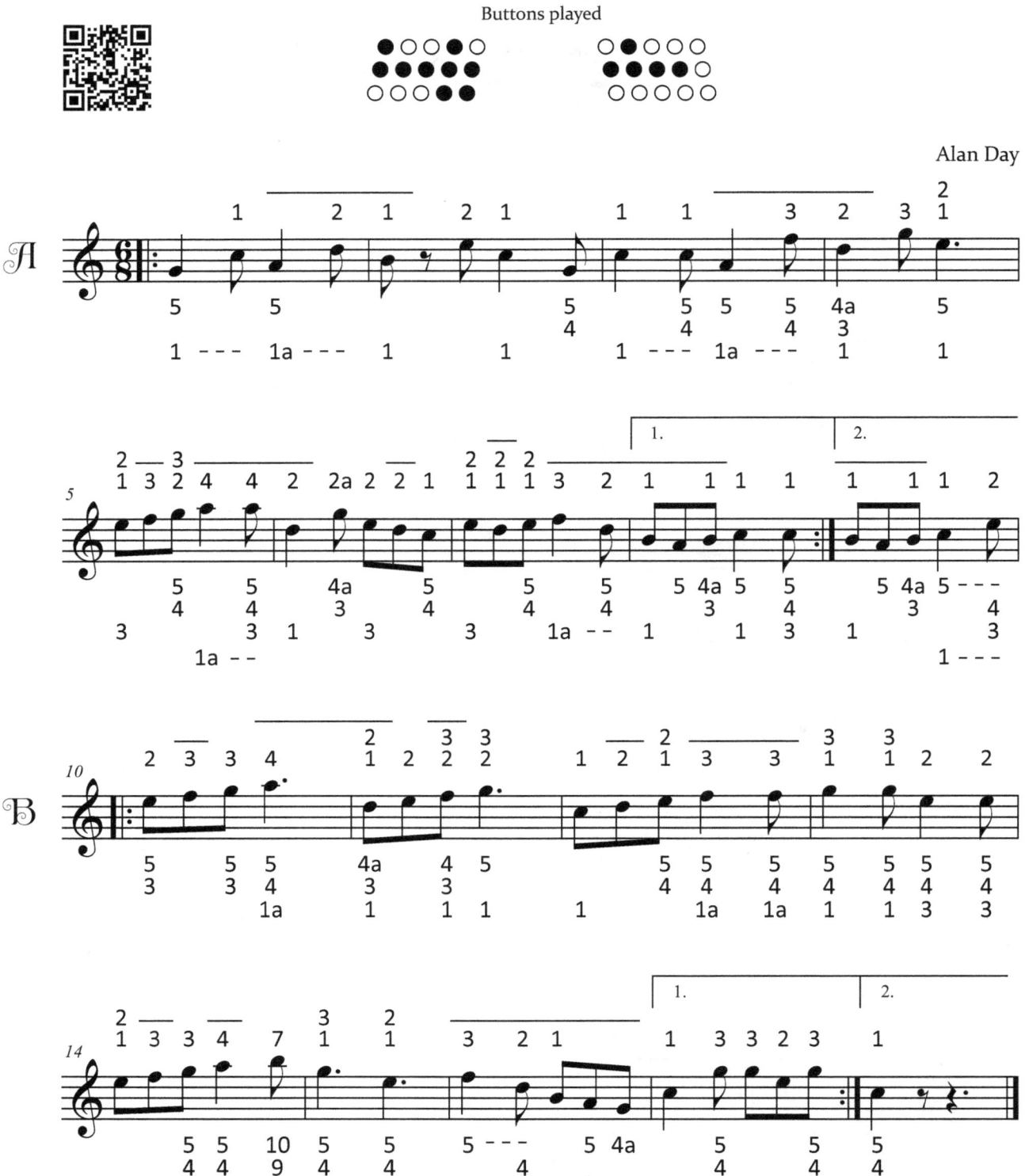

Plasir d'Amour

PLUM DUFF

Buttons played

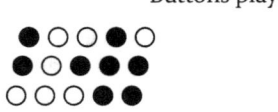
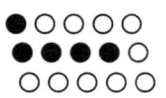

Alan Day

Processional March

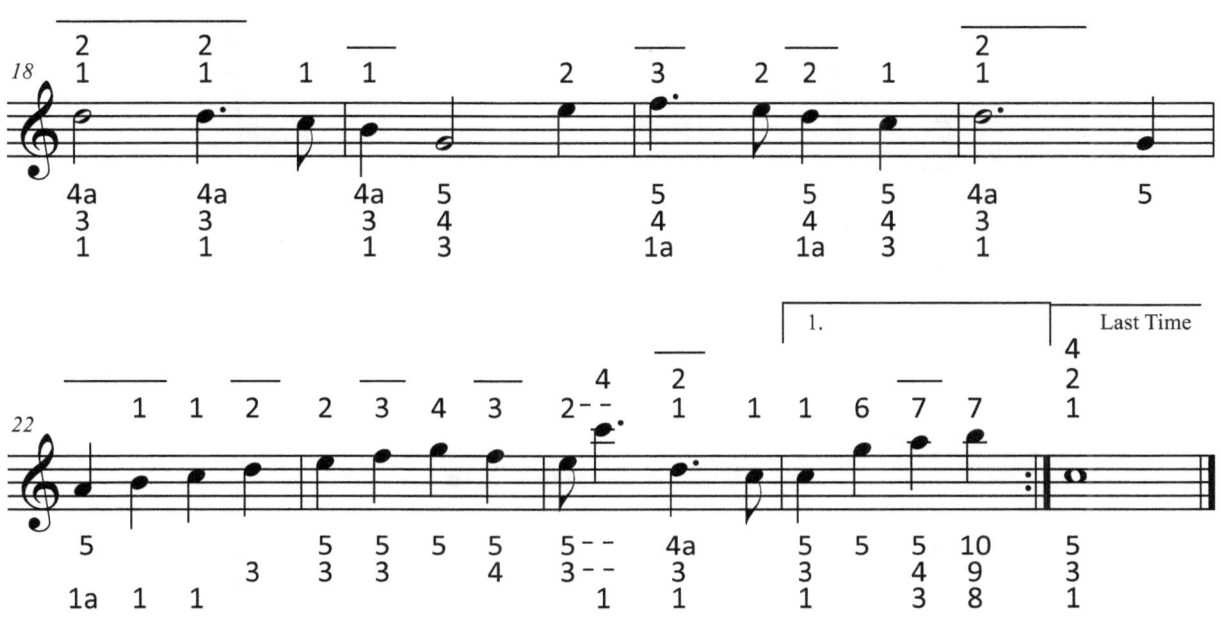

The Queen's Jubilee

Ro's Tune

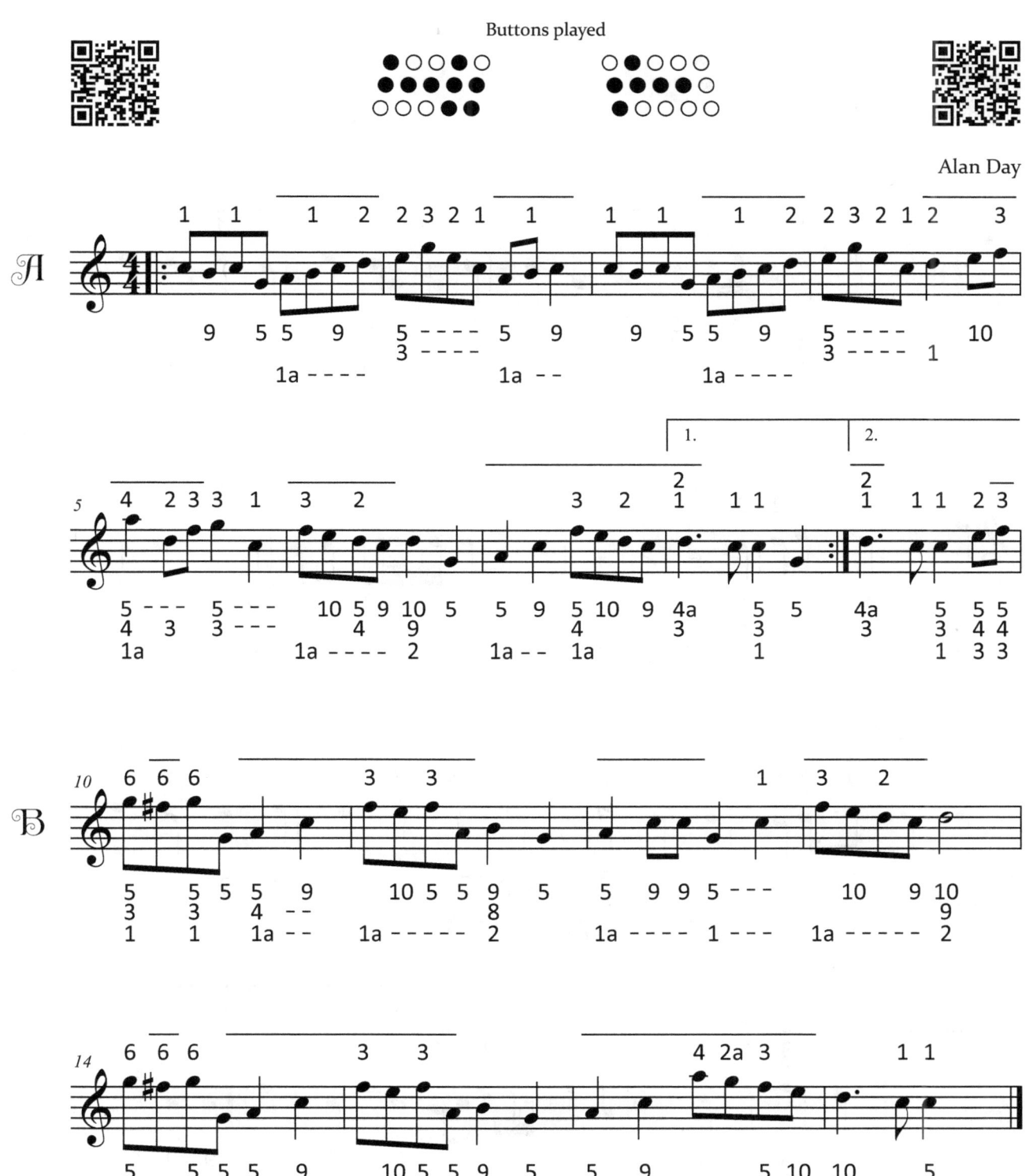

NOTE: Transposed from the key of G to the key of C.

Shingle Street

Sidmouth Polka

Unknown

The Anglo Concertina Music of Alan Day

Snow Flakes are Falling

The Anglo Concertina Music of Alan Day

Son ar Chistr

Buttons played

 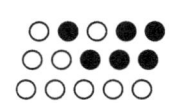 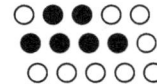

Traditional Breton

Spring Bumbles

Stream to River Flows

The Day Thou Gavest, Lord, is Ended

Buttons played

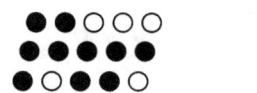

Clement Cottevill Scholefied (1874)

NOTE: Transposed from the key of G to the key of C.

Three Part French Schottische

Buttons played

Alan Day

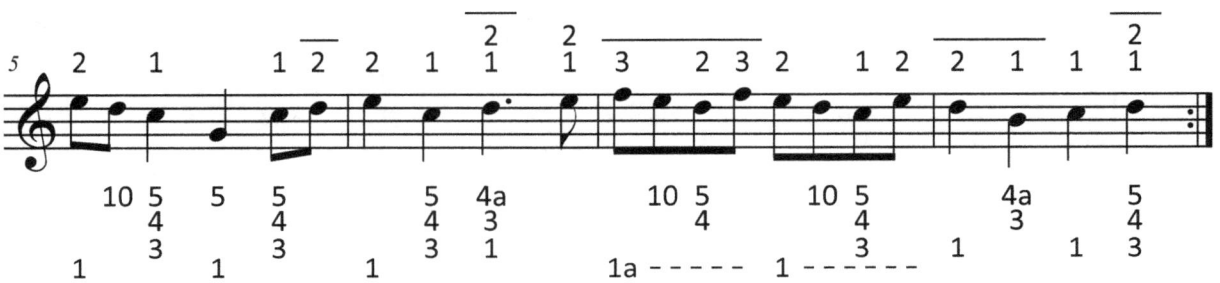

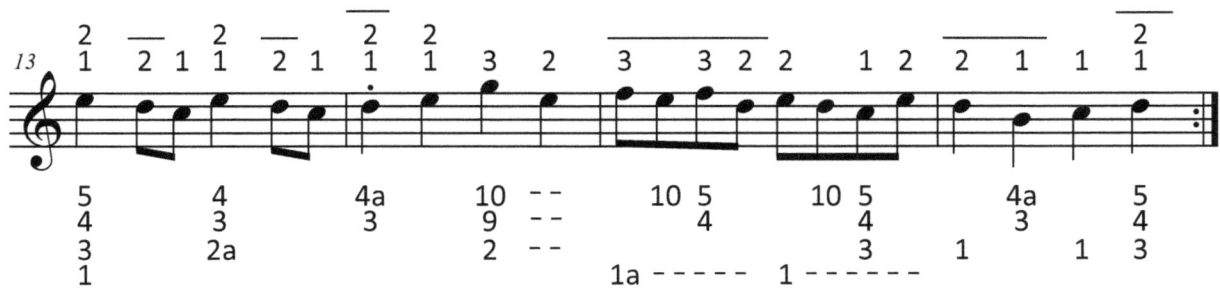

The Anglo Concertina Music of Alan Day

Tom Tolley's Hornpipe

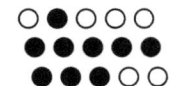

Buttons played

Traditional

The Anglo Concertina Music of Alan Day

Turn Off the Gas Mantle

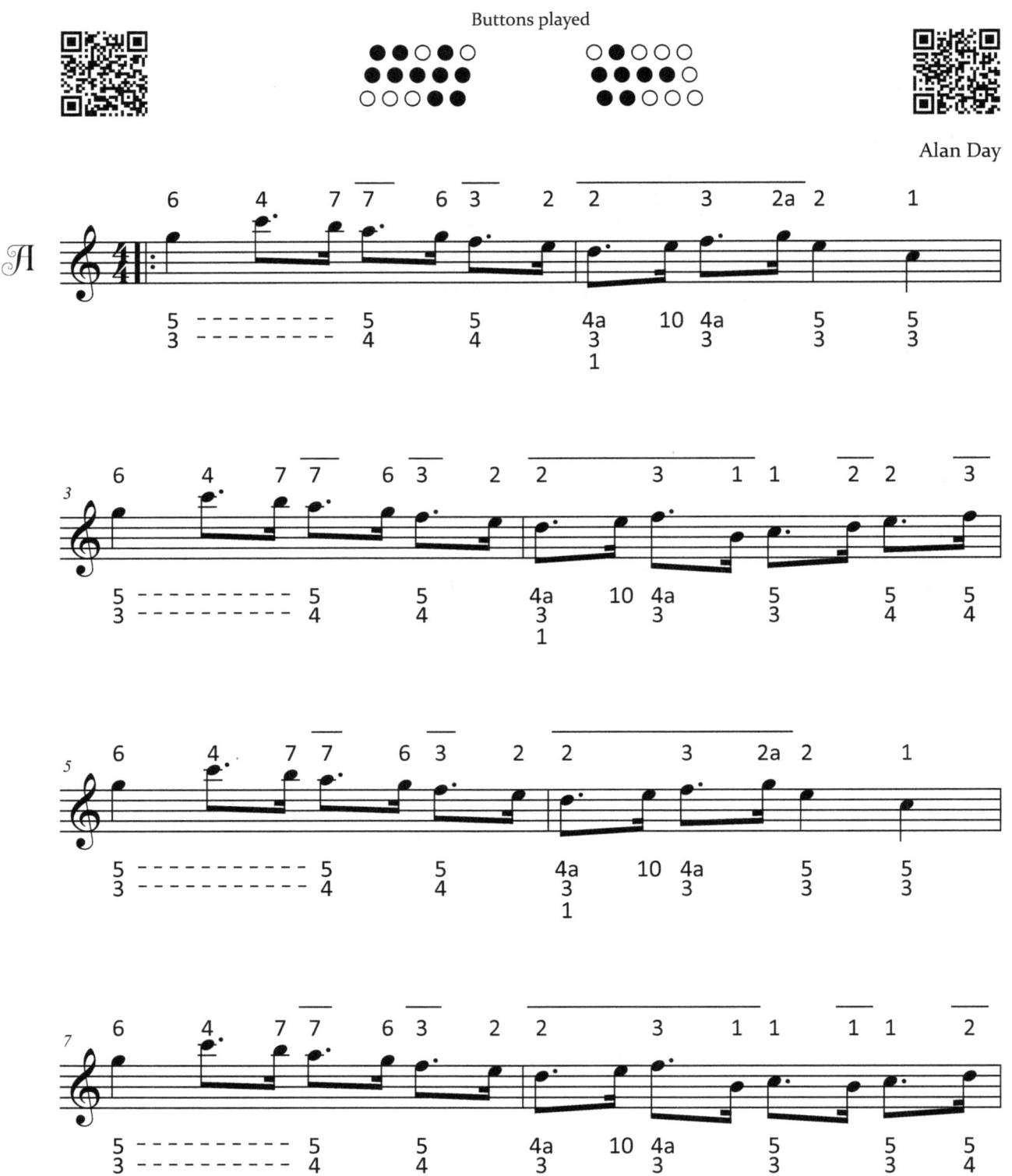

Up with the Sparrow's Fart

Wiggle Woggle Jig

Billy Whitlock (c.1916)

Bonus Tune!

Just as the book was about to go to press, Alan came up with yet one more new tune...

Monsieur Coover's French Waltz

The Anglo Concertina Music of Alan Day

Notes on the Tunes

The Abigail Waltz
A little tune written for my Grandaughter. This is also a song based on the play "Abigail's Party".

Adieu Sweet Lovely Nancy
One from the Copper song collection".

Al Day's Waltz
Written 7 Years ago.

Always Loved, Never Forgotten
Like many of us I lost a lot of friends to Covid and sadly it is still going on. This is for everyone who lost a friend or relative to this virus.

Archie Minor
A tune written for Archie My Grandson.

Auntie Ada's Waltz
Auntie Ada was a second Mum to me and lived in the house forming part of Kemptown Station Brighton Sussex, with my two Cousins Pam and Joyce. I was at that time living in Clapham and on School Holidays I would catch the early Milk Train from Clapham Junction to see them at Brighton. I never slept the night I was always so excited. When Auntie died I wrote this tune for her.

Battle of the Somme
One of the most beautiful War tunes ever written.

The Bees Knees Hop Step
Lovely to hear this again. This has been one of the advantages of relistening to my old tunes and many others in this collection.

Bonjour Mazurka
A tune written with Rosbif in mind. A tune of mine that seems very popular. amongst some Anglo players. A dance that I have just recently learnt after many years of trying to get the hop in the right place.

Chocolate Rabbit
One of my early tunes that started with a base run and thinking "If only there was a tune with a base run like this in it ". Well here it is!

COMMONWEALTH HORNPIPE
Another old revived favourite.

COMMONWEALTH JIG
Same tune but played as a Jig.

COQUETTERIE
A tune learnt from a recording sent to me by Goran Rahm (Sweden), who played it with two concertina friends who got together to play music at his house. I have tried with this arrangement to do as much of the three parts they play as possible.

CROISSANTS ET CAFÉ
A mixture of French and English. One of my favourites to play, I really like the B part.

DAVID STANTON WALTZ
When I moved to Crawley in Sussex, David was one of the first friends I had and we used to go around with a group of friends to all night parties, a trip to San Remo Italy, and many dances including Eel Pie Island, Twickenham. A great dancer. Sadly David had a massive stroke that stopped him going to American Swing Dances and he is now cared for by his Wife. This tune is for him.

FAIRY DANCE
A great tune to play on the Anglo.

FRENCH SET – RONDEAU
This tune starts with a double note and demonstrates using two buttons that have the same note.

FRENCH SET – BOURRÉE
Learnt from my playing with Rosbif and GIGCB.

FUBU WALTZ
There are a few tunes that come along that can make you change direction. This Waltz originally played on two Hurdy Gurdy's I heard at about 3 AM at the Ris Oranges Folk Festival nr Paris ,played by the group "Fubu". It was responsible for my interest in French Traditional Dance Music and not long afterwards our group "Rosbif" was formed. It is here played on a Jeffries Anglo Concertina. I hope I do it justice , as it is a lovely but very unusual tune.

GATWICK EXPRESS
On my sales trips to London I used to park my car at Gatwick Airport and catch the Gatwick Express train which took just thirty minutes to get to Victoria. I must have knocked this tune out either going to or coming back from one of those journeys.

Glastonbury Hornpipe
Difficult little tune to play but well worth it.

The Green Shoots of Spring
An interesting Minor tune.

The Harbour Inn Jig
I go to regular sessions at the Harbour Inn, Southwold, Suffolk, and I wrote this tune for them.

Hollesley Frolic
Named after a village by that name in Suffolk.

I Only Want to Dance with You
Sounds a bit like a 30s Flapper type tune.

In the Toy Shop
A little tune with an Edwardian, street music feel to it.

Jean's Waltz
A tune composed for my Mum. I like the version with Mike on guitar.

Jenny's Hornpipe
A tune composed for Jenny my Wife.

King Cotton (Second Part)
A March that just came into my head from memory. Good fun and very lively.

La Marianne Waltz
A favourite French waltz.

Limey Pete
A tune for gardeners. Composed for *Anglo International!*. From the CD notes: Limey Pete was a fictional character taken from a nursery selling plants near our house and the big sign outside says Limey Peat, and I pinched the name. Not an English/Australian immigrant as some would think. The tune was written on a long journey in the car and put quickly into a dictating machine when I got home.

Little Eavie
A little tune for my Great Great Niece.

Little Mark's Tune
A tune for my lovely little boy Mark. He was a little Angel and sadly died of Cystic Fibrosis (an inherited disease). Played as a hopstep or a waltz.

MANOR ROYAL MARCH
Named after The Manor Royal Industrial Estate based in Crawley Sussex where I worked for a few years. Sounded a good name for a Triumphant March.

MANOR ROYAL WALTZ
Same tune but played as a Waltz.

MARCH OF THE CONCERTINAS
A tune composed for Concertina Day with lots of players joining in this fun tune. A great response from concertina players Worldwide.

MAZURKA GASCONNE & MAZURKA LAPLEAU
These were some of the first selected tunes we played on the very first Rosbif French Traditional music from Central France records.

MONSIEUR COOVER'S WALTZ
Written for my good friend Gary who's hard work and dedication have produced this book.

MOONLIGHT HOP
Another old favourite of mine that I enjoyed reviving for this collection.

MORRIS OXFORD
My attempt at composing a new Morris Dance tune.

OATS AND BEANS
Nice old traditional tune.

THE OLD SMITHY
I really enjoyed hearing this one again. Named after a house we nearly purchased, but cost a fortune in renovations for the people that did buy it.

OLD TOM CAT HOPSTEP
One of my original tunes found compiling this collection. With a touch of Music Hall this catchy tune is now one of my favourites. You can hear my Clapham London upbringing on this one, very Cockney sounding.

PINT OF COCKLES
One of my old favourites.

PLASIR D'AMOUR
Lovely French tune and song. It brings back lots of memories.

Plum Duff
Named after a Xmas type pudding. I like the Fairground Organ style of this one. One of my favourites to play, a bit of Music Hall / Fairground music.

Processional March
A recent tune that I spent a long time composing. I would love to hear this played by trumpets in a big hall, but with all my friends playing it will be good enough for me. Composed just before the King was Crowned. It was not used for the ceremony, sadly.

The Queen's Jubilee
Composed and played in Morris Style.

Ro's Tune
Ro (My Sister in Law) sadly died from cancer much too young. Always smiling. Loved her Basset Hound Dogs. Sadly missed by all who knew her. This is for Ro, with love.

Shingle Street
We often walk our English Setter Lottie along the beach here. The strong current and gales have formed a street of shingle about fifty yards from the beach, just wide enough for the yachts and boats to get through, but it has been said locally that you are not a sailor unless you have been stuck on the shingle overnight. With the East wind it can be bitterly cold in the Winter but normally a very strange and secluded place. Thought to be haunted. By what I am not sure.

Sidmouth Polka
A made up name because that is where I first heard it.

Snow Flakes are Falling
One of my favourite compositions. Like many, this just arrived ,but I am pleased it did. A fast waltz that is lovely to play. Almost a blizzard.

Son ar Chistr
From Brittany. It is hard to stop playing this very lovely tune once you start.

Stream to River Flows
A tune composed after going to a friend's Atheist Funeral, where a little man with a long white beard explained that life was like a tiny stream starting deep in a mountainside, joining up with other streams to form a river that eventually flows out to sea. I have used the base notes to create depth. Quite an emotional tune to play.

The Day Thou Gavest, Lord, is Ended
My all-time favourite hymn. A lovely tune to play.

THREE-PART FRENCH SCHOTTISCHE
A lovely tune learnt from a member of GIGCB who had learnt it on a trip to France. About a year later he said what a lovely tune it was and where did I get it from.

TOM TOLLEY'S HORNPIPE
A wonderful tune learnt from a session in Sussex and luckily I recorded it.

TURN OF THE GAS MANTLE
A good fun tune to play with a nice base run in the B part.

UP WITH THE SPARROW'S FART
I must have got up early to write this one.

THE WIGGLE WOGGLE JIG
A tune learnt from an old 78 record collection of xylophone music. You have to un tangle your fingers after playing this one, which is as much fun as the name. The arrangement has been likened to fairground organ music.

ALAN DAY

Gary Coover

A longtime fan of the concertina ever since discovering British traditional music while in college, Gary was inspired to learn to play the Anglo concertina through the music of John Kirkpatrick and John Watcham.

In 2013 he published his first Anglo instruction book, *Anglo Concertina in the Harmonic Style*, which included tunes from William Kimber, John Kirkpatrick, Jody Kruskal, Bertram Levy, Kenneth Loveless, Brian Peters, and Andy Turner.

The success of this book led to the creation of Rollston Press, which today has nearly 30 titles in its catalog, half of which are instruction books for a wide variety of music especially arranged for the Anglo concertina.

All of Gary's books utilize a simple and popular "play-by-number" tablature system based on 19th century Anglo tutors. Most of the books feature video instruction – Rollston Press was one of the first music publishers to incorporate QR code links that provide video and audio links to YouTube videos and SoundCloud audio recordings.

Concertina Books from Rollston Press

Anglo Concertina in the Harmonic Style

Easy Anglo 1-2-3

Christmas Concertina

Civil War Concertina

75 Irish Session Tunes for Anglo Concertina

A Garden of Dainty Delights

Pirate Songs for Concertina

Sailor Songs for Concertina

Sea Songs for 20-Button Anglo Concertina

Cowboy Concertina

A Garden of Dainty Delights

The Jeffries Duet Concertina Tutor

The Anglo Concertina Music of John Watcham

The Anglo Concertina Music of John Kirkpatrick

The Anglo Concertina Music of Phil Ham

Anglo Concertina from Beginner to Master

House Dance

Chris Droney of Bell Harbour

Handbook of Tunes and Methods for Irish Traditional Music

75 *More* Irish Session Tunes for Anglo Concertina

19th Century Anglo

**Available from Amazon,
Red Cow Music (UK), and other fine retailers**

www.ingramcontent.com/pod-product-compliance
Lightning Source LLC
Chambersburg PA
CBHW081135170426
43197CB00017B/2869